STO

Art in a
machine age

Art in a

machine age

A critique of contemporary life
through the medium of architecture

MAXWELL FRY

METHUEN & CO LTD   LONDON

First published in Great Britain 1969
by Methuen & Co Ltd
11 New Fetter Lane, London EC4
© Maxwell Fry 1969
Printed in Great Britain by
W & J Mackay & Co Ltd, Chatham
SBN 416 04080 2

Distributed in the USA
by Barnes and Noble Inc

1503213

TO JACQUELINE TYRWHITT

in gratitude and affection

Contents

Foreword

My primary acknowledgement is to Professor Johnson-Marshall for suggesting that a series of lectures at Edinburgh University were the logical outcome of too extended a seminar. But my debt to Professor Jacqueline Tyrwhitt goes back further in time and covers a field that she opened for me at Harvard and that really set me on course, if such it can be accepted for.

At a critical stage I have been indebted to Sir Geoffrey Vickers, V C, for views on the current situation that I have found much to my point, and for more detailed help with the manuscript.

The Royal Academy has allowed me to profess my opinions to a limited public which I am happy to say included an attentive grand-daughter; and for the opportunity to recall this duty to its Council I am grateful.

I would like to express my thanks to some readers of my manuscript, including Richard and Margaret Finch; and I acknowledge with a gratitude that extends over a long period of marriage and partnership, the value of the discussions and the encouragement that was given when I stood most in need of it.

E. MAXWELL FRY

List of illustrations

[xiv] *List of illustrations*

The author and publishers would like to thank the following for permission to reproduce the illustrations listed below:

Eulie Chowdhury for plate 1; J. Allan Cash for plate 2; South African Tourist Corporation for plate 3; Ministro della Pubblica Istruzione, Gabinetto Fotografico Nazionale for plate 4; The Architectural Press for plates 5, 16, 41, 58; Aerofilms Ltd for plates, 6, 20, 21; Sam Lambert for plates 7, 18, 52; Henry Moore for plate 8; The Royal Institute of British Architects for plate 10 from *Architecture: Part 3 Design*, produced by Diana Wyllie; Lucien Hervé for plates 10, 15, 30, 34, 36, 39, 40; The Editor, *Architect's Journal*, for plate 17; Cement and Concrete Association for plates 22, 45, 46; Walter Gropius for plates 23, 24, 25, 35; Mies van der Rohe for plates 26, 27; Verlag Gerd Hatje GMBH for plates 28, 29, 37; Alvar Aalto for plates 31, 32, 33, 42; Ezra Stoller Inc. for plate 38; Lennart af Petersens for plate 43; John Ebstel for plate 47; Cumbernauld Development Corporation for plates 48, 49; Crispin Eurich for plate 50; John Donat Photography for plate 51; G. Candilis for plate 53; Kawasumi Architectural Photograph Office for plates 54, 55; City of York Information Service for plate 57; Technical Library, City Architect, Sheffield for plates 59, 60.

Introduction

Though this book could have been written any time in the last ten years the continuity of professional practice in itself would have been enough to stifle the impulse to engage upon a separate work so much more sustained than a series of lectures and articles through which an attitude is given expression.

Then also, the pull of professionalism, the feeling that the cobbler should stick to his last, is as strong as one would expect it to be in this age of specialisation. To write in general terms, to express personal opinions about matters of general concern, runs counter to the demand for authentic opinions dispensed by accredited experts in particular fields of knowledge.

Luckily, I practise an art of which it is difficult to draw the boundaries. Confined strictly to the creation of building form it yet probes so deeply into human needs as to enclose within its scope a dozen separately acknowledged disciplines spanning between science and art. Expanded, as it must be, to include town planning, or as we would have it today, the built environment, there is little that can escape its need for inquiry. If its task is to create a new vehicle for living then not only is it concerned with life as it is lived, but as it will continue to be lived long after the turn of the century, that year 2000 that means so many different things to so many different people.

It is possible that we will not reach the year 2000 in any state to which this book could apply, since we have it in our power to destroy ourselves in the most physical sense of the word. Alternatively, if the present estimates of population for that year hold good, most of the arguments in favour of a civilised standard of living will have been rendered academic by the sheer pressure of people on land, if indeed this pressure has not produced the social evils expected of it before even that year is reached.

These alternatives confine a situation that fills us with uneasiness. So far from seeing ourselves as gods in possession of the secrets of nature which it is in our power to dispose of for the benefit of mankind, at the moment nearly of our acquisition of this knowledge of good and evil, we draw back at the immensity of the consequences that may ensue into a self-examination such as we have not made for centuries.

I do not have to stress the immediacy of the dilemma in which we find ourselves. It suffuses the thoughts of all who have time for thought and can sense a connection between the catastrophes of the last war and the tension of life in a technocratic society since that time.

But it is of all things the most difficult to imagine a plausible and attractive alternative to the life we live, however contingent and menaced it may be. We were, all of us, born well into the story of the scientific revolution that had its origins in the seventeenth century, and habit is now so rigidly encased in conventions that have the force of morality that were our salvation, as it may well be, to depend upon our giving them up, we might find ourselves powerless to act.

The conventions I speak of are not only social, because we have thought ourselves into our present state. Long before the first machine was invented we had entered upon the calculated division of labour from which the machine took over, to particularise and intensify the division without more than deflecting the attitude of mind to which it owed its existence.

But, say my friends, this machine which you appear to invest with a near-animal animosity, is but a tool in man's hands. Science fiction apart, a computer is a digital calculator depending for its efficiency upon what we put into it. To which I can only reply: why are *you* therefore afraid?

I wrote a book called *Fine Building* in 1941* – towards the end, that is, of the year of phoney war and into the blitz. It was a curious period in our lives for we had come through this year of nearly suspended animation, watching with horror what was taking place on the continent of Europe, stirred by, I was going to say, feelings of remorse for what we had allowed to happen, but worse than that, by something that might correspond to the reaction of a man upon whom a disgusting operation had been performed without his consent, an entirely helpless rage at an indignity neither invited nor foreseen.

This period was ended by the withdrawal of the British army from France at Dunkerque, the Battle of Britain, and the beginning of the long aerial bombardment of the country. Apathy and despair vanished overnight, society rose to the obligations of survival, and in this atmosphere of determination for the present and belief in the future I started on my book.

It was, of course, the necessary outpouring of an architect cut off in mid-career, but it expressed, as clearly as I knew how, the spirit of the modern movement in architecture, the coming together of art and industrialism which found its true centre in that extraordinary creation of Walter Gropius, the Bauhaus at Dessau.

I will deal with that period later in the book. It is enough to say here how significant a stage it appeared to be in the evolution of European culture, though whether it was all that it seemed to us, or no more than an historical episode, is for you to decide on the evidence that I will put forward.

I must still make the point that my book was a close reflection of the hopeful atmosphere in which, after the war, the new towns of

* *Fine Building*, Maxwell Fry, Faber, published in 1944.

the Welfare State were conceived, and in considering town planning as the necessary extension of architecture it stressed the need for a comprehensive approach to the solution of the problems of creation and renewal that awaited us after the war. It was a book exactly of its period.

On a troopship to West Africa I wrote a little book called *Architecture for Children**, in the course of which I said that the machine was a sort of fate that we must make the best of, and was taken to task by Walter Gropius for my lack of enthusiasm.

But I hung on to my doubt. I had not seen him since he left England before the war, and in the intervening period the acceleration in the tempo of industrialism, the intensification and the proliferation of mechanism over nearly every aspect of living had become increasingly apparent.

In my own profession, and accompanying a drive to further mechanised building under the pressure of housing demand, a new attitude was developing that set greater store by the group approach to design, on money and management and the lowest common denominator of possible achievement, to the extent that the best architects in the profession could be denigrated as being 'one off' men by a vocal majority supported by the technocratic bias of the authorities.

Necessary and understandable as much of this was, yet there are limits to the extent to which life can be rationalised. It is this rather than the coexistence of the two cultures announced by Lord Snow that stands in need of inquiry.

There *are* two cultures or, at any rate, two approaches to the solution of the great variety of problems to be solved. For one set of problems you use the one, for another the other. Science proceeds by abstracting from the problem what annoys it: art is nothing if not comprehensive. Science employs logic: art is to a much greater extent intuitive.

As we are strongly emotionalised in favour of science and its

Architecture for Children, Jane and Maxwell Fry, Allen & Unwin, published in 1944.

derivative technology, we try to solve every problem scientifically and fail, blinding ourselves in the process to the existence of any alternative. Thus Snow, quite rightly sensing the conflict of intention, would have us merge the two, blurring the edges of what stands in need of separation and definition if we are to measure what set of problems are appropriate to what method of approach.

In the course of the successful development of a rational approach to life, art has become so far depressed as to be denied relevance over wide bands of experience for which its methodology is eminently suited. It is generally supposed to be both intuitive and illogical, and of little account in the practical world amid the dreadful chaos in which we are therefore fated to pass our days, and out of which we must extract the means of salvation in terms of a much closer adaptation to the totality of the circumstances that confine our existence to the future.

So that I want first of all to describe and define the creative process of architecture, in its primitive manifestations, and then in contact with the contemporary scene, to show what kind of an instrument it is.

What this scene is, from what it has derived and what it means to us today, complements the creative process by standing or not standing in need of it. If modern life has little use for a process that is by definition illogical and comes to its most valuable conclusions by intuition, if it prefers to deal only with what is measurable and calculable in isolation from what nevertheless concerns it, then we should know what we are in for.

I have therefore tried to put the dilemma before you as clearly as possible by bringing the story of industrialism and its effects up to the present, and setting beside it the growth, in architecture, of a set of ideas designed to control a nearly equal field of activity by means that are opposite of the other.

This would, if I were a barrister, be my case. But it is not a question of one system versus another. I am not saying that people should go to schools of art and architecture rather than to the

London School of Economics, however tempting the prospect might be.

What might be suggested is the existence, and the necessary and continued existence, of a way of coming to some major problems of contemporary and future life that rely, in the critical phase of solution, on a body of feeling and short periods of intuition. A wide conspectus of relevant events is only fully and deeply comprehended in this way, and thus brought to the surface.

Neglecting this approach in favour of every form of specialisation we multiply and intensify mechanics at the expense of really agreeable living. It follows that, in depressing the miraculous processes of methodical intuition, we banish art and poetry to the periphery and lower the level at which all decisions, whether cultural, scientific, industrial or political are made.

Finally, it is fundamental to this book that art should be recognised as I describe it, that is, as a necessity for, and not a derivative of, life.

Art in a
machine age

1 When the world was younger: the architecture of instinct

It is hard to believe amid this photographic world, that man is a creator with an instinctive sense of form. Yet I hold, against all the evidence to the contrary emanating from reproductive commerce the world over, that this is so: that deep, but available in every man, is the power to respond to the promptings of nature leading him towards harmony.

It could hardly be the case that the creative talent is present in some people and not at all in others, for if this were so there could be no response from the innumerable untalented to the works of the talented few, and talent would stand isolated as a peculiar phenomenon with no binding connection with life in general. Peculiar and mysterious as talent is in the concentrated form in which it manifests itself in the work of a Henry Moore or a Corbusier, what is peculiar is the degree of concentration, not the thing itself, which though essentially mysterious is not peculiar.

The Western world is enormously inventive and creative and has extended, if not its control over, then its power to manipulate the forces of nature for the unique purpose of man. This it has done by means of a methodology properly distinguished by the name of science that achieves its ends, in the main, by studying phenomena in isolation, and though it owes many an advance to flashes of intuition and imaginative hypotheses, prefers what is both material and measurable.

Granted the effectiveness of the means, the ends are now everywhere in question; which is to say none other than that science is being asked to accept limitations hitherto foreign to it and lying nearer to what we must regard as art rather than science. However opposed such a statement appears to the importance now being given to technology as a means of solving current problems, it implies only the need for a different approach at the higher levels of science; the acceptance, that is, of wider points of reference.

But this confusion of means and ends has its reflections at every level in which science is called an aid, mainly because the ruling philosophy, or, more properly, emotion, can imagine no means of arriving at results other than the observation and measurement of phenomena in isolation: it cannot bring itself to believe that a more comprehensive approach could lead to trustworthy solutions. It is not in fact only the ends that are in question, but the means that qualify the ends: the confusion is general.

It is for this reason that I have been driven to examine, more closely than most architects would consider necessary, the successive stages of the artistic process and the methodology upon which it relies, and to investigate an order of art connected with primitive building quite removed from the cerebral and sophisticated issues that can bedevil us today.

In an earlier book I spoke of art as being thrown off from a spiral of sex, a view which I later found corroborated by Rémy de Gourmont in a book called *The Natural Philosophy of Love*,* in which he traces through the insect, bird and animal kingdoms the varying modes of courtship, consummation and reproduction that together represent the universal urge to live. The opening chapters contain these words:

* *The Natural Philosophy of Love*, Rémy de Gourmont (translated by Ezra Pound), London, The Casanova Society.

What is life's aim? Its maintenance. . . . In principle the sole occupation of any creature is to renew, by the sex act, the form wherewith it is clothed. To this end it eats, to this end builds. This act is so clearly the aim, unique and definite, that it constitutes the entire life of a very great number of animals, which are, notwithstanding, extremely complex . . . only in appearance does man escape this obligation of Nature. He escapes as an individual, and he submits as a species . . . Liberty is an illusion difficult not to have, an idea which one must shed if one wants to think in a manner not wholly irrational, but it is recompensingly certain that the multiplicity of possible activities is almost an equivalent to this liberty . . . One must not be gulled by the scholastic distinction between instinct and intelligence; man is as full of instincts as the insect most visibly instinctive; he obeys them by methods more diverse, that is all. . . . If one wishes a unique sole morality, that is to say a universal commandment which all species may listen to, which they can follow in spirit – and in letter – if one wishes, in short, to know the 'aim of life' and the duty of living, it is necessary, evidently, to find a formula which will totalise all the contradictions, break them and fuse them into a sole affirmation. There is but one, we may repeat it, without fear, and without allowing any objection: the aim of life is life's continuation.

In obedience to this universal law all forms of life that need protection in order to perform their allotted cycle have thrown up an endless variety of covering or protective matter in the closest possible collaboration with their associated circumstances. These range from the inconsequential throwing together of the nests of the eagles or swans, through the tightly woven little russet cups of hedgerow birds that coming on when we were young we never again forgot; to the elegant spirally woven caskets of the weaver birds. But in the kingdom of the fish the symmetry we admired in the weaver bird's nest transforms itself through shelly coverings of many kinds into the purest manifestation of accretions obeying laws of progression that appeal to us through the pleasure of recognising what, with no further questioning, seems fundamental to our existence.

The emotions that we experience from that first view through parted branches of the little wren's nest are nearly entirely derived from the similarity between the feathery domesticity of the nest and our own domesticity, and we are happy to avow it. But for the beauty of the spiral forms of the shell we reserve a more strictly aesthetic pleasure, one that carries us into areas of artistic appreciation from which the grosser emotional responses are banished like servants whose continued presence we find disturbing.

Yet they are all of the same material. All these forms we speak of are direct processes of nature. The flower offers itself to the bee, is fertilised and dies as the new seed within it ripens into fruit; but neither bee nor flower have taken thought for the process that joins them; they act the process and it becomes.

Paul Valéry puts this with precise elegance in the following passage from *Eupalinos*:

SOCRATES TO PHAEDRUS:*

Now the tree does not construct its branches and leaves; nor the cock his beak and his feathers. But the tree and all its parts, and the cock and all his, are constructed by the principles themselves, which do not exist apart from the constructing. That which makes and that which is made are indivisible; and it is so with all bodies that live, or that have a sort of life, like crystals. It is not acts that engender them; and their generation cannot be explained by any combination of acts, for acts presuppose living beings.

Nor yet can it be said that they are spontaneous – this word is simply an avowal of impotence . . . we know, moreover, that these beings have need of a thousand things in their environ-

* *Dialogues Vol. IV*, Paul Valéry, Routledge & Kegan Paul, 1957.

ment, in order that they should be. They are dependent upon everything, though the action of all things seems, by itself, incapable of creating them.

But as for the objects made by man, they are due to the acts of thought.

The principles are separate from the construction, and are, as it were, imposed by a tyrant from without upon the material, to which he imparts them by acts. Nature in her work does not distinguish the details from the whole; but pushes from all sides at once, chaining herself to herself without experiments, without regressions, with no models, no special aim, and no reserves; she does not separate a project from its execution; she never takes a direct course regardless of obstacles, but compromises with them, mixes them with her motion, goes round them or makes use of them: as though the path she takes, the object that follows this path, the time spent in covering it, the very difficulties it presents, were all of the same substance. If a man waves his arm, we distinguish this arm from his gesture, and we conceive between gesture and arm a *purely possible* relation. But from the point of view of nature, this gesture of the arm and the arm itself cannot be separated. . . .

What offers the connection between the 'willed' works of man and those of nature itself is the very necessity imposed upon man 'to contrive' that is at the heart of all human creativity.

In order to do so he must collaborate with his surroundings, and it may well be, since both the extent and resources of the world are not limitless, that for us the real secret of the universe is how to read the terms of this collaboration and define its limitations. To the deciphering of this secret we must return again and again; or, failing to do so, risk annihilation.

This relationship is obscured by the seeming success with which we have pursued the search for the secret of matter. It is more evident in the simpler transactions which over the greater part of historic time and in every part of the world provided man's shelter from the elements and unfriendly circumstances and which, for the purposes of comparison, I have classed as 'Instinctive Architecture'.

This type of architecture is to be found in Italian hill cities, in African kraals, in mediaeval roof-scapes, in the arcaded street-scapes of Spain, in the mosaic texture of Marrakesh, in the Amandabele villages of Pretoria. It is everywhere in the ancient world. The very villages we destroyed to make room for the new city of Chandigarh* were the chief solace of our hard-working life there and I will try to describe both their appearance and the feelings they gave rise to, as helping us to a definition of Instinctive Architecture. This term was invented some years before Bernard Rudofsky published his survey of what he calls 'Architecture without Architects'. I am now greatly indebted to this pleasant book but I will continue to refer to Instinctive Architecture as contrasting with the increasingly cerebral art of the present.

These villages of the Punjab plain we would call hamlets. The rich clayey soil supports an intensive agriculture of wheat, gram and sugar. It is not, as an over-enthusiastic French journalist suggested, a desert.

Both the size of the hamlets and their spacing are direct responses to a simple set of conditions with no mathematical exactitude. Men and beasts must fan out into the fields each morning and be gathered in at dusk. What men and beasts with primitive tools can do defines the terrain; where water is locates the village.

At somewhat similar intervals therefore the tracks between the standing crops gather to where the brown earth rises to the barely distinguishable form that shelters a community of seven or eight hundred souls. Seen from the fields it is little more than an excrescence of moulded mud, topped sometimes by the house of the

---

* The capital city of the Punjab, India, designed 1951-54 by le Corbusier with Maxwell Fry, Jane Drew and Pierre Jeanneret (Le Corbusier).

elder or tax collector, and fringed irregularly with trees among which the giant and holy peepul clearly dominates, marking the site of the pond or tank with its temple near by.

An air view would doubtless reveal a still greater degree of similarity between the hamlets, and what is more interesting would show, especially in the season of harvest, the exact connection between them and their agriculture; the extent to which they are as much a part of a process of reproduction as the calyx of a flower is part of a cycle that includes the plant form it decorates, the bee that fertilises it, and the region that invites them to flourish.

I remember once flying home from Africa over Northern Spain and discovering on the ground below a series of beautiful flower-like forms that resolved themselves into villages around each of which some crop was being spread out to ripen or to be threshed. I was too high up to distinguish life: the form only was apparent.

This aerial eye has opened new landscapes to us; landscapes as strange and beautiful, and very often as like, as those revealed by micro-photography. I glance down the sides of unscalable mountains into deeply scored valleys as the tip of Mont Blanc moves under my plane. My neighbour photographs it but is no better off than I. I pass all day over the deserts that stretch nearly unbroken from Delhi to the Atlantic, an endless fantasy of wrinkled earth. Dawn rises over the Sahara like spears of light thrown by an angry rising god: great acts are performed; the Niger river bestrides an infinitude of green as embattled cloud masses, miles high, move upward from the Equator.

It shows us much, this aerial eye, but it may easily become a non-participating experience, or one at least difficult to handle. Our interest in pattern or texture unrelated to other experiences can wane, but on the ground the animal element is regained. Let us, therefore, enter the Punjabi hamlet by way of the track that passes the pond, where the water buffaloes stand submerged to their noses. The peepul tree arches immensely over the water; its roots stretch out gnarled fingers; women gather at the well; a temple bell peals faintly; smoke rises. In the twisting alleys goats press against the rounded mud walls or enter with fastidious tread tiny courtyards where beyond, in deepening shade, the small complications of domesticity are received into white sculptural form (plate 1). Beauty is everywhere, inherent; no more in the courtyards than in the swelling tree trunk; no less in the sweetly arching ironwork of the well-head than in the mild-eyed milk-white bullocks that wait their turn. All is beauty: timeless.

The feeling evoked is one of harmony, as though all the parts have achieved their proper form in relation to the whole and each is different only because nature seldom permits the same circumstances to be repeated. What has remained constant is the common problem, and that it should have remained so, while generation after generation built and re-built, wore down, smoothed over, whitewashed anew after the monsoon, decorated with emblems of the cherished god, with crude representations of the enemy tiger, ensures that each individual solution of the partial problem will approximate towards the whole and bear the common imprint.

Is time, then, the determining factor? And it must be answered 'Yes'. 'Slowness is beauty', Henry Morris* used to love saying as we walked from one Cambridge college court to another, and in slowness and unchangeability common people enter so completely into the terms of their humble tasks that these take on the proportions of a beauty that is godlike because it has become inseparable from nature, yet speaks for the community of man.

I have dwelt long amid the disorganised effects of nature uncontrolled. I know the extensive aimless bush, the wild competitive forest, and I realise how interested I am in man, how compelling I find the humblest of his works, and with what anxiety I search amid the preponderatingly natural scene for his dear, his cherished mark.

On the winding mountain road to Simla, I once came in sight

* Henry Morris, one-time Director of Education, Cambridgeshire, and Founder of the Village College System.

of two great mountain sides. The one, where it was not precipitous, was clothed in trees and was immense, immeasurable. The other was terraced from some level away out of sight in the folding valley below to heights far above me, a dizzying succession of tiny terraces interrupted here and there by small slab-like houses each with its feathery tuft of trees; in the whole a mighty work, but in the detail of its parts, clearly visible to me across the intervening space over which two kite wheeled in endless circles as though time meant nothing, the humblest work of unregarded men.

The first mountainside was, as I have said, immeasurable; it offered no foothold for my sympathy. I could fear it. I could by the same token worship it; but it was beyond my reach. The other was in the human scale, was measurable by reference to what moves us and joins us with nature without deforming our stature as human beings.

Long before I went to India I visited the plateau of Nigeria, where a race of pagans maintained themselves by a meticulous agri-culture of unenclosed fields between the gigantic rocks that shoulder themselves out of the level shelves of fine soil. The women were of noble stature and covered their nakedness with a bunch of leaves only, suspended from a thread, but were to be seen moving across the dramatic landscape bearing long staves, their faces impassive and dignified as in the portraits of the first Queen Elizabeth. These people lived in groups of huts strung together like beads, but com-posed in such a way that the inequality of size as between one hut and another was in some way compensated for, so that the whole, despite its seeming inconsequence, made a perfect necklace. The inequality was in fact an expression of the composition of the group and of its hierarchy. There was a hut for the chief, for his wives, for the wife in labour, for the horse, for the grain, for the kitchen.

Gathered under trees, the little group held itself like a tight cluster of nuts, and each hut was as a nut for perfection (plate 2). Resting on a ring of smooth stones, it swelled out from the base and then narrowed to receive its crown of fine thatch that terminated with a flourish, and the hard fine surface of it was reminiscent of an old bronze casting, something of aristocratic origin.

This emanation of aristocratic feeling, constantly recurring in the works of instinctive architecture, is but another effect of time, of time as perfecting the process of assimilation.

When I first came to West Africa some fifteen years ago, I saw everywhere in pots, mats, baskets, cloth and ornaments evidences for what I can only describe as an aristocratic feeling for design; a high quality of restraint in the ornament, the employment of only the best and most suitable materials, the assumption of profiles of classic purity but filled out everywhere with unhesitant vigour, and exhibiting no trace of vulgarity.

Most of this is fading away because the people no longer know how to want it, but one can still buy in the markets hand-fired domestic pots, made without the potter's wheel, on which with broken glass or some such simple instrument the maker has scratched designs of birds or beasts for all the world like Paul Klee, though as to who came first there can be no doubt, nor much doubt as to what Klee wished, consciously or not, to draw our attention.

I would say only in regard to these African designs that they are not illogical in the half-negative sense in which we have come to take that word. They are no escapes, no intellectual perversions. Having had a long fill of logic we are apt to turn to illogic as a quick cut to sanity. But that is not the way out. These designs are not illogical. Within their setting, they are as rational as anything else in this dream world can be, and it is more valuable to think of them as being simple celebrations: things done for the pleasure of it.

There exists in South Africa a tribe, the Amandabele of Pretoria, that has been saved from extinction by the love of a good man, Professor Meiring, Head of the School of Architecture, Pretoria. I have spoken of the feeling for design running through the range of household articles, implements and stuffs of Nigerian people, and of the harmony of the Punjab village, but here on the inhospitable upland of Pretoria are a people who, you might say, live design.

They are a pastoral people, and choose for the sites of their U-shaped villages the northern slopes of hills overlooking their grazing grounds. Between them and the view are built the kraals for their animals which are also the burial grounds of their elders and important in their folklore.

By custom, which where things remain undisturbed can be described as consolidated good sense, the village plan is always similar. It is made up of units that follow a traditional pattern consisting of a round hut standing in a roughly rectangular court of mud walls about five feet high, but divided midway into a front and a back court or *lapa*; the front for reception, the rear for cooking; and in front of all this a low wall or platform which is a sort of uncovered veranda and social area.

The construction, up to the point where hard labour really sets in, is the work of the men, and the laborious mudding of it is the work of the women who then go on to glorify the mud with decoration that re-lives their lives for them (plate 3). Just as a portrait by Gainsborough seems to absorb into itself everything one could say of the side of eighteenth century England that stood for its dominant culture, so here these vibrant geometric designs in the bold colours of the earth – in blacks, greys and siennas, but especially in blacks – assimilate the dominant characteristics of the Amandabele, their colour, the dress of the women, their implements or ornaments, and if it could be known, their quality as human beings; the proportions, as it were, of their personality.

We came to the village that Professor Meiring has re-established in a cortège of cars bumping over the dirt roads, and we parked them in a group facing the village, these shining aggressive weapons of ours, while we strolled over to inspect.

We strolled over to inspect but I was abashed: the huts were so small, the people so still and contained, so beautiful and superior, I felt that I had no right to invade an intimacy so harmoniously established, and was ashamed of the bunch of cars. For in spite of the boldness of the designs, brilliant on their ground of white, the effect was intimate. It was not a display unless you must count the markings of a snake's skin as display: nor could it belong to that order of natural camouflage which accounts for the appearance of so much that is rare and strange in the animal, and especially the fish kingdom, and which arises nearly always from a need for protection.

These are, as I said, a pastoral people, and this glorification of the dwelling in the likeness of themselves is done each year by the women, searching out the right earths for colours, grinding them and mixing them, and then, miracle that it is, painting them direct upon the whitewash; and not the same designs everywhere, but only the same order of design with invention running through it like a life, keeping it always to the full, unhesitant, and natural.

I was abashed because I had come to know that I could myself design in something of this way and had watched le Corbusier at work re-elaborating his old themes, and I was aware of the capacity to design being a freedom regained; or inversely, that this capacity is normally repressed by the kind of life we lead, driven out by the nineteenth-century way of looking at things still dominant with us, by analysis, factualism, specialisation and the perpetual warfare of commerce.

As if to prove that the impetus to design is regenerated with each new turn of the year and is no stock pattern repeated, I found on some of the walls clear representations of buildings, a motif otherwise absent. The incorporation was successful, but only just so. It had been absorbed with time-won confidence, but it suggested to me the possibility of a breakdown, and I realised to what extent wholeness was necessary to success.

I came away deeply perplexed as to the nature of what I had seen and its bearing on my own life. These people, I said to myself, exhibit, not in these decorations alone, but in their dress, their bearing, their folklore, and, if I but knew it, in the conduct of their lives, a degree of harmonious adjustment superior to my own. I went out to inspect the native compound and was inspected in return by a small sample of something approaching perfection.

And where you find harmony, I went on to myself, is it the outward sign of an inner adjustment? Or only an accident? Yet how can it be an accident, for is this adjustment, this search for harmony in the relationship of our lives to our surroundings not the aim, the conscious aim of the best among us? And is not the opposite of it, maladjustment, the great sickness of our Western civilisation, that fills the mental hospitals and half the normal hospitals, too, that peoples the psychiatrists' couches, creates outsiders and existentialists and sets a permanent frown on the brows of city dwellers half our world over?

As I pondered over these questions, the great wicked city of Johannesburg came into view, the place where cynicism takes the place of sense, and fatalism is the only religion; the existential city of Johannesburg.

Now surely, I said, there can't be two measurements. Either what I have seen is significant and what I see in Johannesburg is, on the whole, without permanent value, or I'm just a tourist being shown the African reserve.

But what is it that tourists seek if it is not this very thing? Chartres and Stratford-on-Avon, Florence and Rome, no doubt. But do they not leave their technocratic centres in search of what is textured by time, lichened, rough, hand done, innocent? Of what, for so little longer, in whatsoever places still sequestered, remains 'unspoilt'?

Read this of Gerard Manley Hopkins:

Glory be to God for dappled things –
For skies of couple-colour as a brinded cow ;
For rose-moles all in stipple upon trout that swim ;
Fresh-firecoal chestnut-falls : finches' wings ;
Landscape plotted and pieced – fold, fallow, and plough ;
And all trades, their gear and tackle and trim.
All things counter, original, spare, strange ;
Whatever is fickle, freckled (who knows how?)

With swift, slow; sweet, sour; adazzle, dim;
He fathers-forth whose beauty is past change:

*Praise him.**

I bring back from West Africa little animal toys made of gut and fur which the children treasure and never lose. I brought my daughter a bag made of cheetah skin which her children and her friends stroke involuntarily. Why is fur still of value, like gold and brandy? What is it our womenfolk seek to comfort themselves with?

I search about for clues, for qualities and attributes, and everywhere find positive evidence of what below the level of architecture is rich with the value of something germane to it.

There are the temples of Greece isolated for inspection but denuded of what they rose from, the residual form of vanished conditions and emotions. We only partly understand them. But when we read the *Symposium* of Plato the conversation about love springs living from the page, Alcibiades reels into the party with girls, and is wonderfully funny with Socrates. This we understand without difficulty.

The Instinctive Architecture of the fishing villages of modern Greece, with their sculpture of steps and roofs and their frescoes of whitewashed walls, we as easily understand, though it comes to us in unbroken succession from the ancient past (plate 5). If we put them all together – the temples, Plato and the lowly villages – we may begin to understand how the Acropolis grew more complicated with time and association and particular consideration of this human and that divine factor, and recognise the connection between the continuity of common form and the emergence of the stresses of loftier motives finding definition in sculpture and architecture.

The African forest-people built, so far as we know, no great temples. Yet they too felt the need to rise above the common form, itself still beautiful, to the perfection of objects for kingly and priestly use that transcend their purposes, and become works of art so firm

* *Pied Beauty*, Gerard Manley Hopkins.

and yet so persuasive that it is now they and not Praxiteles who fertilise the imagination of Henry Moore and Paul Klee and fill the void in our Western culture.

One senses in all this an upward movement from the living compost in Instinctive Architecture to points of clarification, particular emotions distinguishing it and raising it, temporarily, to higher levels of art. Given the maintenance of a fixed set of conditions Instinctive Architecture will cling to its achieved form with tenacity, but let these conditions favour some such excess over equilibriums as lifted the Athenians to dominance over the islands, and at once the particularisation takes place, though connected always with its environmental background, its grass roots, as Whitman called them.

I have been describing examples of what appears to occur in all parts of the world where conditions are favourable and have isolated for sustained inspection some definite virtues inherent in orders of building verging upon architecture that are in simple connection with the facts of their creation over long periods of time.

The simpler the connection and the less the intervention of thought-based action, the closer the building will approximate to natural form and the less will its parts be differentiated.

It has always struck me on seeing the profile of New York or looking down upon it from above that, in its general aspect at least, it too is a sort of Instinctive Architecture of a debased kind explained in terms of external pressures. Unlike Paris or the West End of London where the form of what is built is the result of thought and selection, New York seems at first merely chaotic and later resolves itself into a crystalline formation not unlike the Giant's Causeway or Fingal's Cave. Given the constriction of Manhattan Island and the financial pressure of growing America concentrated on it, skyscrapers will shoot up accordingly; densely in the downtown and 42nd Street areas, less so elsewhere; and neither those who finance these skyscrapers, nor the architects of them, will work to any concerted plan or pattern, but will respond blindly to the pressures of overwhelming necessity.

Seen from a distance New York responds thus to my definition of Instinctive Architecture. Exhibiting an absence of thought-based action and composed of rectilineal growth-units differentiated only by height, its association with human beings would not at first be guessed at. The comparison with canyons, mountains and the like comes naturally to normal people, who see its beauty as a demonstration of nature rather than man.

At close range the simile fades for lack of supporting detail. Much of what was beautiful at long range – beautiful as material over which sun and cloud chase each other – becomes, at close range, without meaning. Unlike the form as a whole, which could not but expose the giant forces of nature moving through it, the detail of it fails to make explicit the purposes either of man or nature, and as artefact is insignificant.

It would not do to leave this freak example of New York to close a description of Instinctive Architecture drawn largely from my own experience. It leads me to the comparison that must be made between the Instinctive Architecture as described and another equally anonymous class of building that constitutes the greater part of the industrial urban scene of the nineteenth and early twentieth century.

The rumbustious eighteenth-century slum of Hogarth's 'Gin Lane' hardened into what came to be known as the 'bye-law street' which I described in *Fine Building* as follows:

> The bye-law street is the mathematically exact product of a set of minimum standards defining the widths of streets, the distance between the backs of parallel rows of houses, the angles of light, the width of service passages and so on. By comparison with the standards hitherto obtaining they were pure sweetness and light, or at any rate irrefutably sanitary and hygienic. The only other virtue I will allow them is that they adopted the rigid technique of absolute standardisation, which should have enabled them to offer higher standards of many

1 . . . 'tiny courtyards where
beyond, in deepening shade, the
small complications of domesticity are received into white
sculptural form.'

8 Family group by Henry Moore,
1945-49. Tate Gallery, London.
'. . . a sort of mindless state, the
features reduced to the barest identification of humanity, as though what was
human in these rounded monoliths
looked out helplessly from their
earth-bound stony captivity.'

kinds of household equipment. But this virtue must be partially withdrawn because standardisation was so materially interpreted and was not in essence generous.

These tracts of bye-law housing, extensive as towns, are dominated by a crude idea of reproduction reduced to its simplest terms as repetition of similar units in response to an overriding principle of materialist economy.

It is clear from a random example of back-to-back overcrowding in Everton Heights, Liverpool, preceding the bye-law streets in date, that theories of industrial economy were a cloak to aggressive acts of self-preservation by power-owning classes at the expense of the workers.

Be that as it may, I have still to describe the phenomenon as it continues to exist in considerable quantity, to see where it is to be placed in the hierarchy of building, and what it has otherwise to say for itself.

The unit as it finally emerged in the typical 'bye-law' street was a small two-storey terrace house, equal in width to a staircase hall and a front parlour, with or without a bay-window (plate 7). Its materials varied regionally, subject to a rigorous economy, but the extent of its variation diminished as the machine brickyards of the Midlands and North West superseded locally-made bricks, and the slate quarries of North Wales drove all other forms of roofing out. It was not without ornament, and the inspiration for such ornament as it allowed itself in capitals, keystones, terracotta ridge-tiles and finials, and in the stained glass panel of the front door, was, I regret to say, supplied by none other than John Ruskin.

In the example I offer you may even admire, for there is no accounting for tastes, the carving of the capitals that support the brick arch of the door. It derives possibly from Ruskin's *Stones of Venice*, though other details may be taken from books on English mediaeval art.

Moreover, they are all made by hand. Houses of this period owe less to direct machine manufacture than one might suppose. They are rather the product of piece-work which is the machine idea applied to human labour.

There then is the little house unit, tricked up in deference to the Man of Art and solidly equipped with something more than the necessities of life. There it is, as unlovable as it is possible for a man-made thing to be; and this loveless foundling, begot in greed and sin, of parents unknown is reproduced in rigid lines of street after street disappearing into the smoke-obscured light of a day that knows no season, in undifferentiated and godless boredom (plate 6).

Now, though we recognised in Instinctive Architecture a degree of sameness in the parts of any one manifestation, it was never boring; however extensive it might be we could regard it all with pleasure and sympathy.

The difference between the two can best be explained in terms of the kind of emotion brought to each. In the former a small problem of building of which the terms were well understood was solved in a human sort of way to the general satisfaction of an integrated small society, with everything of a piece, everything done by members of the group for whom it was done. The latter is guided by a one-sided reason, a dubious emotion, and a feeble understanding of the facts bearing on design.

The decorative motifs are lifted from some book because Mr Ruskin shamed them into it, and though he also explained to them the difference between variety and contrast and pure repetition, they did not listen, being too deeply grounded in the materialist economy of an age whose god was the machine.

So these areas are exactly and interminably repetitious. The same house unit with the same capitals from the *Stones of Venice* over square miles of parallel streets that end abruptly without terminal feature may be interrupted to accommodate a factory or a workhouse as representing the beginning and end of life, but continue thereafter in geometric rigidity to the limits of economic exploitation.

No attempt is made to approximate to any social grouping whatsoever because in fact none exists, and if now after the passage of nearly a century some community of the street has arisen from the association of families – kinship is the term used – this must fight against the mechanical pattern, a fungus in its joints lacking the strength to establish its own form.

Before we leave this horrifying period we must note the success with which the system of thought expunged every element – 'all things counter, original, spare, strange' – that Gerard Manley Hopkins celebrated; all texture, all irregularity, all emotions of pleasure and delight.

It would seem that Instinctive Architecture has had its place in the world wherever and whenever life was simply organised in some communal basis, but has shrivelled away from the first impact of industrialism and is now a negligible factor.

The lower levels of present day society barely contribute to design of any sort. They contribute to the infinitely diversified and specialised labour of the industrial system as employees in factories, and in the highly planned building industry where their opinion is seldom asked, but they are without knowledge of the process as a whole. Their likes are therefore divided into working and non-working or leisure periods with the minimum connection between the two, and they suffer accordingly.

Members of this class move into petty shopkeeping, speculative building, garage owning and the like and their lack of comprehensive understanding of what they are about is responsible for the hideous aspect of the roadsides.

They are the fringe of a disorder that affects society at large, but they offer a comparison between other and earlier groups of humble people who seem to have been so much more in possession of what makes for wholeness and human dignity.

Artists have reacted to the situation in a manner that gives point to this study of Instinctive Architecture. They first broke with the whole idea of classical and Renaissance painting as no longer reflecting truths valid for nineteenth-century life. The Impressionists sought their subject matter in the common people, in peasants, washerwomen, prostitutes and, affected as they were by scientific ideas, attempted to break colour up into its components.

As one movement succeeded another, realism and its laws of perspective, the discovery of which gave such life to Renaissance painting, was replaced by intensely subjective experimentation into every means of expressing the subconscious and instinctive aspects of life to which, in Picasso's Avignon series, African primitive art made a decisive contribution.

The work of Henry Moore shows a direct return to primitive sources. His earlier sculptures consisted of pebble forms, hollowed out and sometimes strung with wires, with usually some breathing holes, as it were. He never deserted the human figure entirely but retired to a sort of mindless state, the features reduced to the barest identification of humanity, as though what was human in these rounded monoliths looked out helplessly from their earthbound stony captivity.

In later works, as for instance the King and Queen figures, he allowed himself a nearly naturalistic delineation of a hand or foot, but reduced the faces to inhuman beaks looking blankly out; however his reclining figures have with time taken on the aspect of pagan goddesses.

In our present period painting at large has rejected the human figure in favour of what is called abstract art but is really one or another method of exploring the subjective unconscious, of drawing up from states of chaos, as in action painting, what can be found to express an artist's reactions to his situation.

Most of the work I speak of comes from artists working on their own or in defensive groups. Organised patronage virtually ceased with the eighteenth century. Objective science and its offspring, Rationalism, had little use for art other than as a means of consolidating wealth, and in return artists have found little to celebrate in the society that rejected them. Deprived of a social structure to which art might adhere, they moved successively backwards towards a primitive world of instincts and feelings, even to the edge of the sensual chaos that appeared to Henry Adams* to be the direction in which science and the world it commanded was tending; and in all this still rejected, still unconnected with any society they could acknowledge.

What emerges from this short study of instinctive architecture is that, in following his instinct towards successful survival man seeks harmony. He seeks an adjustment between his life and the conditions that surround him, which finding he celebrates with art, never losing at any point the vital connection between hand and mind.

What little remains of this order of building and making in the world today is being ousted by the industrial reproductive system, which is severing forever, or for as long as we continue to exalt rational thought over all other kinds, the link between man and his surroundings, leaving him bereft in a world with which he has less and less communication.

If, though continuing to use the machine for the performance of major tasks of reproduction, we can both organise our man-made environment in collaboration with nature and as a massive work of art on the scale that we must deal with, and at the same time offer the assuagements of art at close range, we may perhaps be following the line of successful continuation. But for this we require a change of heart that is not unlike the return of humility before the facts of life that St Francis might have demanded of his followers: a return to the study of the motives which underlie the important activities of modern life.

*The Education of Henry Adams, Henry Adams, Constable.

2 Eupalinos: the conscious architect

Let us return to the quotation from Valéry's *Eupalinos* that came early in the last chapter, and dwell for a moment on the rich and vivid image of nature in its never-ceasing act of continuation. 'She never takes a direct course regardless of obstacles, but compromises with them, mixes them with her motion, goes round them or makes use of them . . . as though they were all of the same substance.'

And the architect, by contrast, in approximating to nature, must proceed by acts of will, must take thought before imposing his will on the materials out of which he constructs; and yet be bound, as surely as he must live and die, by laws and principles that bind the natural world.

The unconscious or intuitive builder, whom I called the Instinctive Architect submerged in anonymity, appears now as an indistinguishable agent of the natural process, interposing but a feeble will, guided so directly as he is by the pattern of events in which he finds himself. But the circumstances that confront an architect today interpose between him and the natural world a system based essentially upon abstract conceptions of mechanical perfectibility flourishing in a medium from which human considerations have been largely removed.

We are indeed under pressure to produce a mechanical explanation for architecture, if that were possible, and constantly to defend our judgement and artistic certainty along a wavering borderline of art-science, heavily charged with statistics, graphs, and a dubious moral flavour, for 'the technique of science, like that of industry, has become a thing in itself; the one veils its object, which is nature, as the other defeats its purpose, which is happiness'.*

But the process of architecture is the opposite to the practice of science, and their methods are antipathetic. From first to last architecture is a comprehensive art and joins with science only at science's higher levels where it appears to its more optimistic ministers to be on the threshold of the creative act. It would not, I think, be presumptuous to point to the enormous difficulty in which science finds itself when contemplating the idea of comprehensiveness, and to state by contrast that this idea is the working method of artistic creation. There must be admitted a difference in attitude to the material upon which the two disciplines are employed but, that said, our problem lies rather with the effects of the scientific attitude embodied in its offspring, industrialism.

Since the process of architectural creation is at the heart of my argument it must be described in detail. Its mainspring is intuition, which Santayana describes as 'a broadly based activity; it engages elaborate organs and sums up and synthesises accumulated impressions'.† It sounds like a computer. It would be nearly a relief in some quarters if it were. But, definitely and finally, it is not.

It has three stages: a long period of preparation and dedication that comes only to a head at the instance of design; a moment, one might say, of creative intuition; and a further lengthy period of correction and adjustment to the formed idea.

Of these stages the first is the longest and the least understood. It could be taken to include the whole of an architect's life that is tapped at intervals for whatever will produce a design, though the

---

* 'Revolution in Science', *Five Essays*, George Santayana, Cambridge University Press, 1933.
† 'The Prestige of the Infinite', ibid.

long life itself is more important than the moments at which it is tapped.

Then also, it is not only the length or the activity of the life that is in question, but its quality for the particular purposes of architectural creativeness: it is for what this life will bring in terms of feeling and imagination at the moments required of it.

Works of art – of architecture, of drama, of sculpture, it matters not which – are valued by us because they explain the meaning of life to us by defining the form in which it can best continue. They must therefore contain, along with anything else of which they are composed, some long-enduring element that projects them into the future.

We need not regard this element as being eternal. It is unnecessary to talk about eternal truths, which are very difficult to understand, but we can recognise two principles involved: one of change and another of conservation, of permanence or endurance.

The principle of growth must realise itself in form, and the continuity of growth is therefore interrupted to produce forms that are maintained over periods that differ according to the circumstances in which they take place; sometimes for so long as to give the illusion of permanence; at other times, of which our time is one, with a rapidity bordering upon the chaotic.

A successful form would be one that comprehends the greatest number of usefully enduring elements in the ambient circumstances. Art is very much concerned with what endures. It follows from this that no art can be narrowly particular, for what endures is never the particular but something more general that has only its reflection in the particular.

Our concern, as architects, is limited by what we deal with. You will not expect to learn from our buildings of human passion, and Othello and Hamlet have no place in them. But it would be an illusion to regard them as something different. Life expresses itself in many ways and Hamlet would mean nothing to us now were he not embodied in a work of art, the play; and the sequence of that play, the character of its language related to the end in view, the timing of its scenes, the pace of its action culminating in the final tragedy, make a structure that is to be considered as a unity in itself, nearly apart from the sense of it: as a sort of building, with foundations, pinnacles and a vast echoing hall.

What we have to deal with – and in no sense is it less important than what Shakespeare had in hand – is the slower drama of weight and mass, the downward pull of the earth from which, as humans, we derive our sense of balance; space, which involves our relationship with surfaces and masses; form, revealed by light and shade and shot through with the character of texture; contrast and variety; time; and rhythm, that final mystery coming up from the animal centre of our being, which to understand, and to control, is the noblest office of our art. There are also, as I am to point out later, a set of feelings evoked by form, ranging from the edge of terror, through constriction and its opposite, release, to calm and reassurance.

This drama of earthiness, the struggle of things involved in human destiny, has as its warrant the service of one or another human activity, of which architecture is an envelope that outlasts the immediate purpose. The activities change with time, burgeoning here and fading there, and resisting change very much in accordance with the significance of the architectural shell they formed about them in the period of their greatest activity.

There are two sides therefore to consider; the one dealing with what we call, for want of a better word, inanimate things (though it is the life in these things we seek, and they are not therefore inanimate nor separate, but involved); and the other, which is the community of man in all his varied activities.

All that is to be enacted of them in any one building, but all that this building can mean for purposes human or divine, must issue through the brain and heart and bowels of an individual. That is the indisputable fact. Is a group the sum of its individual capacities? Or is it its mean denominator? Is society the supreme distillation of all that is best in it applied to all its acts? Or is it the mean average of its intentions saved by the greatness of individuals? There lies the dilemma of the historians, who continue nevertheless to write of individuals because in the notable among them the history of the race is written. Or if you prefer to scale down the individual contribution, then you may see the historically individualised figures as being the accidental vehicles that invite and contain and give recognisable form to the blind pressure of natural and social growth.

This individual we may now think of as the dedicated architect, and I have to imagine him first as a person of feeling, since feeling is the key to comprehension, as later it will dominate design; and this feeling, the emotional intensity with which he experiences life, I see directed or exposed in three directions; towards human activity with an accent upon its organisation; towards nature in the widest sense of the word, and including its manifestations in art; and inwards to the workings of his own nature, the instrument through which all experience must pass.

His relationship to society is both that of an agent and a mentor. As an agent he obeys instructions concerning the practical arrangement of space and the disposition of useful objects as closely as his skill allows him, and he is judged by his success in these practical matters, and by his economic expenditure of the money involved.

This side of his work attaches itself to everyday life with a closeness not to be found in any other art. It is *of* the market place, the workshop, the family; it is drawn from the very midst of human activity. Each time an architectural problem is proposed a human activity must be described in detail. But such an activity may be described from a variety of standpoints, and if the work is to prosper there must be some measure of agreement between architect and client as to the interpretation of the description: that is to say, it is better if the architect belongs to the group for which he works.

Yet it may happen, as it has constantly in my own history, that there is a genuine deficiency of understanding of the problems on the part of a client, due to an inability to read plans, to imagine space before it is created, or to see the connection between architectural cause and effect.

Then there exists an instinctive urge not to change an environment once established which, in a country of fixed institutions such as England or France, is a barrier to any interpretation for which no precedent exists, and leads to compromises that drain off the energy upon which a work of art depends.

Of the same protective or defensive nature is the instinct to run with the herd, to keep up with the Joneses, and not to be seen as falling behind in the struggle for existence. This latter is easier to deal with because it involves the spirit of emulation; there is always the chance of there being someone better than the Joneses, and as an attitude it is not without energy.

But it is clear that at the very outset of the creative process and in this workaday establishment of the programme upon which any architectural problem is based, there is an element of selection, appraisal and imaginative interpretation on the part of the architect that is drawing him into his own creative atmosphere, in which already he must act both as agent and as critic of the terms of his agency.

Many architects doubt their capacity for this office of critic. I have often been asked what I would do if a client's requirements ran contrary to my views on architecture. Such questioners should not be architects; their doubts are only worthy of shopkeepers.

But this power to interpret is a measure of the intensity with which an architect experiences life, and not only that part of it that is thought to concern architecture. The more profound the sympathy, the more delicate the apparatus by which he receives all kinds of impressions, the better the interpretation he makes.

When John Vanbrugh came finally to his life's task of producing a fitting architectural environment for English Whiggery, what wealth of experience had he not already amassed, and how clearly he saw and felt the essence of his problem. 'State, beauty and convenience' he declared to be the creative basis for his work, and his clients hastened to agree.

But there are circumstances, the happiest possible for his art, when an architect is acted upon by society. No longer an observer, no longer interpreting by his own lights what he feels to be his instructions, he becomes absorbed into society by emotions which he shares with it in their entirety, so that his every creative act is reinforced by a tide of feeling that is carrying everyone with it.

In such circumstances was Chartres Cathedral built. The Abbot Haimon of Saint-Pierre-sur-Dives, writing to the monks of Tutbury Abbey in England in the year 1145 told, as Henry Adams remarks, of the spirit which was built into the cathedral with the stone.

> Who has ever seen! – Who has ever heard tell, in times past, that powerful princes of the world, that men brought up in honour and in wealth, that nobles, men and women, have bent their proud and haughty necks to the harness of carts, and that, like beasts of burden, they have dragged to the abode of Christ these waggons, loaded with wines, grains, oil, stone, wood, and all that is necessary for the wants of life, or for the construction of the church? But while they draw these burdens, there is one thing more admirable to observe; it is that often when a thousand persons and more are attached to the chariots – so great is the difficulty – yet they march in such silence that not a murmur is heard, and truly if one did not see the thing with one's eyes, one might believe that among such a multitude there was hardly a person present. When they halt on the road, nothing is heard but the confession of sins, and pure and suppliant prayer to God to obtain pardon. At the voice of the priests who exhort their hearts to peace, they forget all hatred, discord is thrown aside, debts are remitted, the unity of hearts is established.

Henry Adams continues:

> Of course, the Virgin was actually and constantly present during all this labour, and gave assistance to it, but you would

get no light on the architecture from listening to an account of her miracles nor do they heighten the effect of popular faith. Without the conviction of her personal presence, men would not have been inspired; but, to us, it is rather the inspiration of the art which proves the Virgin's presence, and we can better see the conviction of it in the work than in the words. Every day, as the work went on, the Virgin was present, directing the architects, and it is this direction that we are going to study, if you have now got a realising sense of what is meant. Without this sense, the church* is dead.†

The building of Chartres offers us an example of the nearly complete identification of the architect with the group he serves, and, when that group is dedicated to a lofty ideal, the finest architecture results.

There is today a relationship of a kind that involves a large group, the occupants of local government housing, with another group that serves it, the architectural departments of the authorities concerned. Now the former, because of its size and anonymity, is without direct representation to, or communication with, the latter, except and occasionally after the event. The latter, because of its resultant isolation, must make up for this lack of intimacy, first by consulting a body of precedent, constantly under revision in the light of new experience, that concerns both the broad principles and the details of accommodation and the means of achieving them; and by using its imagination.

It would not be thought that so tenuous an arrangement would work, yet from my experience of the London, and now the Greater London Council, the operations are performed with enthusiasm and humanity, size even being to some extent a measure of success.

The explanation is not far to seek and stems from the revolution in feeling dating from Ruskin and Morris, and burgeoning under Ebenezer Howard and Raymond Unwin and his companions in the

* Chartres Cathedral.
† *Mont Saint-Michel and Chartres*, Henry Adams, Constable.

idealistic garden city movement, was given an entirely new lease of life by the modern movement of the thirties in England. This gives this purely municipal function, wherever it is active, its emotional faith and its body of humane principle. Within the normally and formally constituted body of local government this faith would have withered had not the architects' creative methodology been incorporated into government departments with the release of the imaginative faculties concerned, so that young men and women could enter the service in the knowledge that their talents would be valued and that they would follow the full creative cycle from inception to completion of their works.

There is probably no other country of which this is so true, and I remember insisting upon it before taking up our work on Chandigarh, knowing that the repressive codes of conduct set up by the British in India would trust no engineer further than they could see him, and no architect whatsoever.

As a result of this sensibly liberal attitude of British local government acting under the influence of Ruskin, housing in this country has been both more humane and sensitive than elsewhere. But it is now in some danger from the pressures of political economy and big business in mechanised building, for whom the properly idealistic background of housing means little.

Earlier in the century, when modern architecture was working out its salvation, I was one of a group of architects devoted to the development of an architecture for a new society finding its clients among another group equally devoted to a new idea of living in towns. I watched these two groups fertilising each other with their ideas and enthusiasms until it would be hard to see from which side new ideas had emanated. We are a long way yet from the state of mind in which Chartres was built, but one side of our life tends in that direction.

Modern architecture could never have been divorced from its social morality. In seeking its way towards a valid expression it had perforce to analyse the circumstances in which it had to operate and doing so was brought into contact with every other line of inquiry – with sociology, anthropology, hygiene, medicine and so on. It joined forces with movements that already had respectable histories of re-formatory action, and for this reason was able to adopt a clear attitude towards housing and town planning, humanistic but with an accent upon the therapeutic value of light, air and verdure.

The first block of working-class flats I did with the late Elizabeth Denby was the result of just such a fusion of interest, merging ideas of urban living and architecture to the benefit of both.

Architecture is, or should be, society's environment, and it is inevitable that a search for a valid architecture should concern itself with the whole organisation of living, of living in towns especially; and thus architecture, from being as it was, and still too much is, a decoration on life, becomes a moral force. It cannot accept an environment in which its virtues of coherence and rationality are extinguished, but must put forward its ideas of what constitutes a coherent plan of living in the emerging circumstances of its time. It is therefore nothing if not social in the highest degree.

It follows from all this that the architect, without necessarily adopting the distinctive role of doctor or priest, acts or should act, in a similar capacity, for if in ministering to society's need for build-ing he verges towards the man of affairs, his ministration itself draws upon experiences in which the world has little place: one eye cast towards the drains, the other to the heavens! As the human problems become more artificial and complicated, and the means of solving them come to depend increasingly on the products of industry, his contact with nature both as he experiences it in the external world and as he recognises it in himself, may provide the chief element in his work capable of evoking sympathy.

It is in the first case an attitude that places him in a proper relationship with his surroundings. The beauty of a landscape he knows so well is constantly evading him as one deep impression succeeds another. At one time it is the shadow under the heavy oak trees transfigured by light upcast from the grass, fresh wetted from a summer storm; at another it is the immensity of a winter night sky, the bare earth dark and silent below.

He knows that these receptive moments are among the higher experiences of his life and that he may not hope to reproduce more than a tithe of what they represent to him; yet it is with impressions of the same order that he is concerned as an architect; it is with form and texture, the fall of light, with veils of space, and with mass and weight that he must create his own structures, and in no other surer way can he strike a path through the artificial substances of building to the vital processes of nature from which, essentially, they proceed.

Then further, in the detail of nature, lovingly apprehended, he will find every form of structure suggested, as in no other way could the engineer Luigi Nervi have been led to his so original structures. Their value would appear to lie in their origin in nature itself, just as the attempts of Cézanne, repeated during a lifetime of painting, to render truly the structure of the country around Mont Sainte Victoire – its structure revealed by colour, texture and light – confirm his originality as a painter. When we turn to art it is a substitute for nature and it will tell us, but with what pleasure, with what addition of human emotion, what we have found out for ourselves but will now find with the painter's eyes, and never afterwards forget. It is always there to be found afresh, and each generation of painters and architects comes to it with new problems to be solved, in new circumstances; and to those who come in humility it will offer its secrets.

Frank Lloyd Wright wrote at length of what he called 'Organic Architecture', and drew deeply upon natural form. I believe indeed that his work will repay study from this aspect of its originality as architecture alone. But to have gone so directly to organic form is not necessarily a chief virtue, and could be a defect. That all form is interpenetrated by nature, that all structures, however artificially conceived, conform in one or another way with natural law, leaves no separate place for a separate organic architecture.

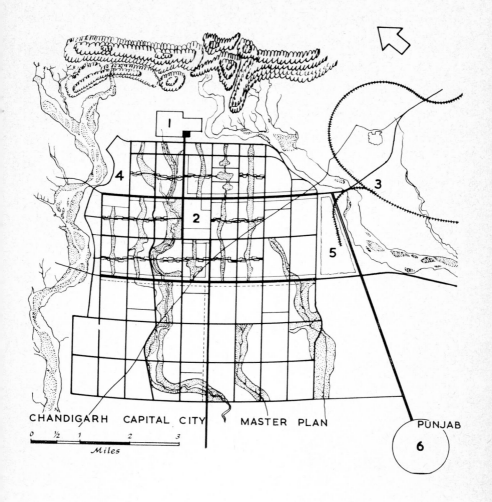

CHANDIGARH CAPITAL CITY MASTER PLAN PUNJAB

0   ½   1   2   3

Miles

9 The plan of the capital city of
Chandigarh, Punjab, India,
confined by its lateral river beds
and low hills to the north-east.
The railway (3) and a central
river bed, which is now a park,
fixed the main lines of the sector
grid, with the capitol at the head
(1) and the city centre (2) at the
crossing. To the east of the
capitol, the river bed has been
transformed into a lake.

above
10 The High Court, Chandigarh, by le Corbusier. A building resting in the shade of a parasol, its roof.

above right
11 Layout of the central areas of Ibadan University, Western Nigeria, showing the single orientation of most buildings in a concentrated pattern of inter-locking function. Later buildings consolidate the campus.

below right
12 An early photograph of the Mellanby College, Ibadan University, showing part of an east-west block of students' rooms, diversified by falling levels and blocked by a north-south running dining hall.

UNIVERSITY COLLEGE, IBADAN, NIGERIA

THE OFFICE OF MAXWELL FRY, JANE DREW AND PARTNERS   SCALE: 200 FEET TO 1 INCH

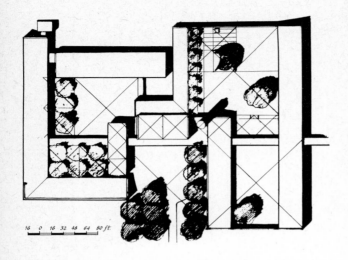

16 0 16 32 48 64 80 ft.

13 Plan of Wudil Teacher Training College, North Nigeria, showing the design structure of multiple squares.

14 View of Wudil Teacher Training College, North Nigeria, from the entrance court.

The forms of nature are parts of a process of growth from one thing to another, the form itself nearly always impure as it mingles with and makes use of its surroundings. Thus the Seagram Building of Mies van der Rohe may represent a much closer approximation to organic form in the jungle of New York growth. Its structure may be impure, it may appear to stand champion to a technocratic idea not easily associated with nature, yet in its time and place as an item of technocratic process it may be nearer the natural order of things than the over-suggestive configuration of the Guggenheim Museum in the next avenue. And if it is then it would be due to the greater intensity of its architect's apprehension of nature and the disciplines of art.

I would not make light of the difficulties of preserving this contact in the contemporary world of technics. Mies van der Rohe speaks of the task of making his architecture significant as being no child's play; but he gives technics no higher place than they deserve, regarding them probably as an inevitable material of growth to be used with impartiality and absorbed into art.

Modern building rests upon a technocratic base. Its function and its form are dictated by what science has produced to solve the problems of urban life at high concentrations, and we are its beneficiaries. But our ends are not technocratic, we do not seek the technocratic life, but only life itself.

Thus it would appear irrelevant to enlarge upon the complexity of the technical foreground of architectural creation. It is indeed so complex and diffuse as to require interpretation by specialists in its many fields. It gives rise to an ocean of printed matter and offers a constantly changing choice. It is moreover interlaced with all sorts of peculiar emotions, many of a low order, and is subject to pulsations of fashion and herd instinct.

But it is never more complex than a work of architecture can be. However many systems of heating exist only one may be chosen for any one building. Out of whatever imaginable multiplicity of choice offered, only one of each kind may be chosen; and this choice is dictated not only on technical grounds and economy but by over-riding ideas concerning life and art.

So let us pass on to consider the inward-looking aspect of the architect's apprehension, his reaction to the closest and most direct manifestation of nature within his experience – himself.

Rémy de Gourmont has stressed the overwhelmingly instinctive composition of the human psyche and the compulsion to reproduce, to continue life, that bestrides every other activity even to the edge of intellectualism. Two things seem clear: first that it may be acknowledged as the single driving force of life and art, and that even so intellectual an activity as architecture must be penetrated by animal emotions and instincts which it would be foolish to disavow; and second, that it would be wise to regard all art as a process of change realising itself in a succession of variably enduring forms.

Thus an artist is served not so much by introspection as by a necessity to protect his instincts from contamination by society. Delacroix says somewhere in his Journals that an artist should be fit for the best of drawing-rooms but should not frequent them, as he, alas, was wont to do!

The long-haired self-regarding architect would therefore be as wide of the creative mark as the brisk executive in black coat and striped trousers, both of them diverting energy to the building up of an attitude to the world that involves some collaboration with it, and losing thereby something of inner tranquillity and simplicity of out-look. Over the course of centuries architectural form has created its recognisable symbols and become intellectualised, and as scholarship has codified them and history sanctified them they have taken on a life of their own which we refer to as architecture, and which seems in the process to have become external to us, something to be con-templated coolly and cerebrally as capable of manipulation to this end and that, and especially as the basis of critical analysis. But the more we think of architecture in these terms the further we get from its essential purpose, which is to reveal the meaning of life to us, to fortify our hold on life, and to celebrate in ways open to it the drama of the life process, as you will find more fully developed in the next chapter.

There may not be any means of making an architectural scale of emotional responses, though this is what architecture is about, and this is why architecture intellectually conceived fails to move us deeply and why so much of apparent talent in the world fails to produce an equal quantity of robust architecture.

And it explains the miracle of Chartres, the deeply moving emotional force of that society that speaks to us in the so original forms of its architecture, sculpture and glass.

The presentation of the inner simplicity that makes such creation possible has nothing of the 'holier than thou' attitude towards life. Rather the reverse; rather the normal than the abnormal. But neither the set attitude of any society nor the prescribed formality either of the intellectual or the businessman nourishes what makes the dedicated architect; the essential is not to spurn the animal in us, for it is holy. It is as simple as that. Only the way of the world leads us to forget it.

Just as there appears to be no way of codifying the forms of architecture in accordance with their emotional response, so there is no means of calling them up by the operation of the intelligence. We are speaking now of states of mind and conditions of flux. But we are still speaking of the process of architectural creation, and pointing out and underlining and insisting upon its value to humanity as resting upon the depth of the responses it is capable of evoking and these depending to so great an extent upon primary instincts.

I have hinted at the instinctive basis of so much of the emotion we bring to the enactment of the architectural process.

Where it remains fresh and strong, architectural design moves unerringly towards forms that have their correspondence in nature broadly considered, and the incidence of form, the rhythm that makes buildings sing, comes like a living pulse, fresh and original. Whatever stands in the way of this emotional response diminishes its flow, as for instance the rise of scholarship, following the exact recordings of Greek buildings by the architects Stuart and Revett, killed the flow of Georgian fantasy; as, in our own time, the insistence on a pure essence of industrial prefabrication would destroy the possibilities of any compelling architectural rhythm. The subtle variations and the relative impurity of Mies van der Rohe's construction reinforce the supposition.

I have spoken at length on this period of preparation for a work of architecture as being in essence the life of a dedicated architect, and as being concerned with the feelings he is capable of entertaining for the world about him and the people in it, including himself. They are the feelings of one who hopes to create buildings and cities, and are different only in kind from those of one who hopes to write an opera, a tragedy or a poem. Their particular value to us lies in their connecting two worlds that have become divorced from each other: the scientific and industrial, and the world of art.

So I may now go on to speak of the creative act itself, the second stage which I defined as a moment, one might say, of creative intuition.

It would not be too far fetched to describe the process as a sort of falling in love. Having said which I will describe what could happen following the commissioning of an architect for a particular work, let us say, for the University of Ibadan in Nigeria, since it is myself that I have really to talk about when I try to describe what happens at this stage, and the particular experience has left a deep impression.

The early appraisal of the facts of a commission is a work largely, but not entirely, of the intelligence, since from the beginning facts are mingled with personalities and everything has its emotional charge. But there is lot of ordinary common sense involved in the early stages of sorting out the accommodation and deciding roughly what goes where. A University such as Ibadan, with its staff housing, is self-sufficient as a town, and rests upon the successful analysis of a mass of factual considerations concerned with access, circulation, drainage, aspect, foundations, before even the disposition of university function is involved. The primary search is for an anatomy acceptable to the conditions, the structure of a set of functions that analysis is in the course of making clear.

In this lengthy process the structure begins to appear as a series of hazy alternatives without as yet any definite personality. But avenues are closing as the multiplying impressions call for comprehension, and decisions are made, not, be it noted, as the direct response to analysis, which must very soon have served its purpose, but from a growing fund of feeling that is already transmuting the straight-line facts of the matter into the comprehension of an idea.

One can also sense, in this ante-room stage of the process in which the creative intelligence is groping towards a solution, the need to systematise, to create systems, general or particular, out of the unordered facts coming forward. This faculty for constructing systems, for sensing their existence in varying arrangements of events, is indeed basic to the creative mind in whatever sphere it occurs.

The generalised feelings bearing upon the early conception of Ibadan concerned the idea of the community and the awareness of climate and site, and these feelings began to colour the increasing number of decisions concerned with the emerging plan and the fabric of its architecture. I need not dwell upon just how elusive and indecisive a university body can be, or how partial and unbalanced a programme of accommodation devised by those who profess to unlimited knowledge in individual spheres of influence.

Dealing with these so human difficulties and with a steady resistance to new architectural ideas, with the less controversial but necessarily complicated assortment of fact, as one after another consideration closed one after another avenue of decision, the moment of recognition approached, and how like it was to what Stendhal, speaking of the process of falling in love, called the moment of 'crystallisation', the moment when what was hitherto factual in the presentation of the object of affection becomes idealised under the pressure of an emotion in full tide.

I find that students lack the patience to wait for this moment. They have an idea, and it is usually someone else's idea, before they have had time to assimilate the conditions in which an idea may be born.

But there are instances when it lies there ready for its opportunity to be born, as was the case when, in a Rest House on the Simla Road in the village from which Chandigarh got its name, Corbusier, with three of us, more witnessing than assisting, created the plan of Chandigarh in about four days of concentrated work, but substantially in less time than that (plate 9). Starting on a clean sheet of paper, and proceeding from broad analysis to synthesis following a method of working that was his gift to C I A M,* he laid out the main lines of the city, from which we never after departed. To do this he had rapidly to assimilate several major sets of conditions, one of which was that the city had to be on the flat without expensive structures of any kind, rigorously economical. Another concerned the topography of the site with its two bounding and one intermediate dry river valleys, the foothills immediately to the north, and the great Himalayas closing the north-eastern view.

He had to assimilate these factors, but the rest, the kind of sector or city block appropriate to the plan, and how it could be subdivided, how motor traffic could flow without prejudice to good living, what should belong to the state, what to the city, where a city's head should be, where its stomach, what size its limbs, how it should be fertilised by nature – all these things he had long pondered in his journeying about the world, had put to the experiment of his schemes – so few realised – and had mixed up in his thoughts with the art and poetry and living that occupied his time as an utterly dedicated artist-architect.

Therefore when he came to the 'moment' of those few days in which the plan was born he created with cheerful certainty, and what

* Congrès Internationaux d'Architecture Moderne.

would have been for many a hard-won struggle had all the appearance of an idea released. It was beautiful to behold!

Another instance: it took some time for him to realise the climate of Chandigarh with its period of intense heat in which the achievement of shade is only a beginning towards that of comfort. But he noticed how in Mogul palace building the roofs acted as parasols to outdoor living and from this he conceived the idea of a building resting in the shade of a parasol, the air passing between the two, and the idea took such a hold on him – he could not talk too often about it at the time – that it became the dominant idea of the High Court building expressed with the utmost force of his imagination already strongly affected by Mogul architecture (plate 10).

Returning to the University I ought now to speak of the crystallising of the architectural idea; the so-called 'moment' of the creative act.

It was some months after we had first seen the site, had assimilated the survey of levels, and wrestled with only limited success with the correlation of the programme of needs. It had been decided among us, and it was a decision of importance, that our nucleus of building should be highly concentrated to avoid needless movement in tropical sun and rain; we had realised the necessity of orientating all habitable buildings in a single direction so as to invite the prevailing breeze to pass through them, and by the same token to create a sort of perforated architecture that would fulfil this condition. We knew the limitations of the drainage scheme as well as those of the water supply. We had stone, but little else for building needs, and we knew how much we must rely on concrete as a building material, and how far, initially at least, we could rely on the capacity of available contractors.

We had, in fact, passed through the analytical phase and were held up by questions of taste and by an all-round blockage of personalities and feelings, the consequence perhaps of our general isolation in the midst of an undertaking of which so much still remained unclear. Then, one morning, under a canopy beside the pool by the Principal's bungalow, impelled by I know not what certainty of impulse, I started designing the first residential college as part of a total scheme that was quite clear to me, and working at a high intensity I produced by the next day a set of drawings in which all the principles enunciated, and a large part of the feelings not yet expressed, were exemplified in a comprehensive design which was immediately accepted in the spirit of 'why did you not do this before instead of arguing so?'

The point of all this is to suggest the variety and the scope of what is entertained by an architect at the moment of creation. What is to be particularly noticed in each of the examples mentioned is that a wide conspectus of fact and feeling, in the case of the plan of Chandigarh a very wide one indeed, is grasped, as Whitehead has put it, 'into the coherence of a single idea'.* What was hitherto separate and unrelated, what was cold and inanimate, has become fused under pressure of an imagination working under stress, but not necessarily labouring, into an entirely new form that contains the essence of all its former parts; that has used them, mingled with them, fused them and minted them as warrantable currency for the future.

The idea that results from the process in the form of an artefact, a building or a city plan, is not only coherent (which is to say, a unity in itself, resolved in its parts) but is an aspect of the 'concrete' that owes its success to what it has succeeded in including rather than to what it has had to exclude in order even to begin to consider its problem. It is a newly created artefact deeply impregnated with the environment in which it was composed; or putting it in another way, although it is a single and coherent work of art it mirrors in its various aspects a wide conspectus of events both in place and time.

It has also to be remarked that this intense period of creation can pass beyond the boundaries of conscious direction. It is not only the case that writers or painters or architects possess the faculty of recalling under stress what out of their experience is of service to the matter in hand, but rather that at some moment in the process they hand over its direction to less conscious faculties and the material itself takes over, suggesting the nature of oncoming steps. It is not

* *Adventures of Ideas*, A. N. Whitehead, Cambridge University Press, 1933.

so much that everything is fused as that the emerging form of what is to be is being dictated or embodied by some inner necessity of the material itself.

Thus Pasternak, at the apex of that sad story when Dr Zhivago* is caught up in his final creative session in the lonely house at Varykino, speaks of the process:

> Finally he got into his stride and, carried away, he started on a new poem.
>
> After two or three stanzas and several images by which he was himself astonished, his work took possession of him and he experienced the approach of what is called inspiration. At such moments the correlation of the forces controlling the artist is, as it were, stood on its head. The ascendancy is no longer with the artist or the state of mind which he is trying to express, but with language, his instrument of expression. Language, the home and dwelling of beauty and meaning, itself begins to think and speak for man and turns wholly into music, not in the sense of outward, audible sounds but by virtue of the power and momentum of its inward flow. Then, like the current of a mighty river polishing stones and turning wheels by its very movement, the flow of speech creates in passing, by the force of its own laws, rhyme and rhythm and countless other forms and formations, still more important and until now undiscovered, unconsidered and unnamed.

This idea, which has become a design, a work of art in embryo, has now to be protected though the lengthy period of its being prepared for execution. If it contains as much of what concerns it as an idea as the best of Nicholas Poussin's† paintings do, it will pass through the ordeal unscathed. More than this, it will come through refined, to the genesis of its personality will be added character.

It will be recognised that my description of the creative process is

* *Dr Zhivago*, Boris Pasternak, Collins and Harvill, 1957.
† Someone once asked Nicholas Poussin to what he owed his success as a painter to which he replied: 'I have never neglected anything.'

a generalisation of the extent to which successful architects may diverge from it. I was told once of an architect whose only method of working was to make awful little sketches, which were worked on by assistants and then chopped about until they got to what he wanted, and were then by no means negligible. Denys Lasdun said to me that he 'sweated' architecture out of his system, meaning that it felt to him like a labour. But I recognise him as a dedicated architect, so that his labour may not be quite as he describes it.

The first period has been described as one in which the dedicated architect makes himself aware of the currents of life, and refreshes himself continually in nature and in nature's substitute, art. This last period is a re-descent into the world in which the architect is in his workshop with his assistants about him, the centre of a great coming and going of technicians, experts, engineers and estimators.

It is the moment to emphasise the practical nature of the art of architecture which keys it so securely into current life. Whatever ideas it may have about the future, and however unconservative it may be in essence, it is bound in the first case to be usable by those who will immediately inhabit it; and secondly, to use whatever is immediately available wherewith to build it. It is irrefutably rooted in the present.

In the early days of developing a new architecture in England our ideas, which were in advance of public opinion, had to struggle not only with obsolete bye-laws and bewildered local councils, but with an absence of such materials and techniques as would make them possible. We had to invent new techniques and use materials in a new way, but we could do so only with the co-operation of the building industry as it existed, and the industry, responding through its brighter spirits, gradually adapted itself to meet a new set of demands upon it.

This is entirely in accordance with the principle of growth that mingles with, uses, adapts and finally transforms the material of its environment, and is what makes architecture so certain an agent in the process of civilisation.

The creative period having thrown up an idea in the form of a building, this latter period must confirm it in practice, and build it in fact. The idea, was not, as we have seen, conceived *in vacuo*, but came trailing clouds of associations and assimilations drawn from the life of its creator. These now stand to be tested in the workshop, where they will suffer the rigours of practicability and cost, and suffering them must still, and even because of their testing, convey the essence of the idea itself. Thus this period is both a collaboration with and a criticism of the building industry; we have an obvious need of industry, but only as it helps us to perfect an idea that issues from an individual.

This makes nonsense of group or team working, as on the whole it should. Such combinations are effective at secondary levels concerned with technical matters subservient to the leading idea, and they are apt to spring up where a set of ideas is in such apparently common use that new ones might appear as nearly destructive of its usefulness. Otherwise team working is no more than a new expression for the necessary combination of interests out of which a work of architecture is created, and in which the contributions, so far from being equal, are diverse, sometimes contradictory, and in need of being harmonised by reference to a leading idea, which is of necessity architectural.

Yet we have still to deal with the bogy of technique and in particular with the industrialisation of architecture itself.

The argument or threat so commonly used is that if architects continue to be long-haired, industry will take them over and do the work itself; to which the answer is that if industry were to do so it must assume the same order of responsibility to society as architecture purports to do, and thereby become an art, and industrialists artists. I see no objection to that. But the virtue of the industrial process lies in reproduction, that is, in the unlimited copying of fixed models of production suited to the industrial process. It suffers therefore from inflexibility and tends towards uniformity of supply and demand.

But supposing this virtue, as it must certainly at the moment be counted, were to change; supposing that industry could become flexible and find the adaptable joint for which Mr Rodney Thomas* has for so long been in quest; supposing that instead of costly and elaborate tooling up for a new model it could offer infinite variety over a wide field of products: then half our labour will have disappeared and we should be in the situation in which Vanbrugh and any other eighteenth-century architect found himself, that is, with a reservoir of skill capable of transmitting any architectural idea likely to arise, with every variation possible, and the full disciplines of the art thrown fairly back where they belong.

But that is not yet the case, as the Hertfordshire school system clearly shows. The struggle between the virtue of the industrial system to reproduce fixed models, whether they be as small as a screw or as large as a whole panel of building, and the architectural virtue which is to create organic unities, despite the talent and enthusiasm of a gifted band of architects, remains unresolved. In the 'window wall' system of cladding buildings the day goes on the whole to industry, with a consequent loss to architecture.

Whether or not industry succeeds in providing us with the means of doing it, we are still under the compulsion of creating architecture satisfactory to the soul, an expression which can attach itself to the highest tenets of art or the most erudite and esoteric theory of the good life, but which one could prefer to regard as the expression of de Gourmont's admonition to reproduce, to continue, which better suits my views and allows us to take industry wholeheartedly with us in evolving new forms by whatever means lie open to us now and, more problematically, in the future.

We run inevitably into a curious intermarriage of architectural theory and industrial practice in introducing the module to this account of the process of architectural creation. The module has come to be associated with prefabricated building, which is a natural development of the industrial system. The idea behind the modular

* See *Architectural Design*, August 1955.

system, as it has come to be known, is the manufacture or pre-fabrication of fixed parts of buildings which can be put together to produce architecture. Though this subscribes to the principle of industrialisation in encouraging the mass production of piece goods, because of some virtue inherent in the module it is likely to be beautiful.

The virtue from the manufacturing and building side is clearly one of repetition, and from the architectural side the repetition of similar units is an element of design. But we must be clear as to what we are about. The reason for using a fixed module is to ensure that the parts of building, whether of structure or equipment, shall conform to sizes recognised by industry as adaptable to repetitive manufacture, since this is nearly the only economy that industry understands. There is a mathematical basis for good design that involves the repetition of similar elements, but it is not the same thing as the industrial module we speak of, for there is a mathematical element in beauty, yet beauty is not the direct product of mathematics. The result of fixing modules is to limit articulation.

Now there is a region of architectural aesthetics and speculation, a very tanglewood of theory and mysticism to which all manner of men, from the loftiest minds to the simple-minded, are led by the light that streams from the Golden Number to seek short roads to architectural perfection.

The Golden Number or the Golden Section is a natural phenomenon that can be expressed mathematically as a ratio of balanced equality between two magnitudes $\frac{a}{b} = \frac{b}{a+b}$ or $\frac{0.618}{1} = \frac{1}{1.618}$, or as a spiral such as is found in certain shells, or as a series of expanding rectangles. It is a natural phenomenon and would appear to be an expression of the principle of growth that connects mathematics with architecture, so that one could say with le Corbusier that all art is mathematically based.

This series of numbers exists, and there is evidence to point to its exemplification in natural form. It has been calibrated in what has been known as the Fibroni scale and gives us in two-dimensional proportions the Golden Cut. Le Corbusier* has gone further in cutting into this scale at the height of a large European man to work out his celebrated Modulor which attempts to provide an instrument for securing the established harmonies of the golden section in three dimensions. He had hoped that it would not only be an instrument for design but would establish an harmonious series of dimensions of service to industry in its necessary work of standardising and mass producing.

But there is a fatal distinction between the mathematical evidence for the Golden Number and the visual effects architecture seeks to produce. These effects are not only visual but are subject to normal emotional and mental interpretation. Architecture finds its way to the mind through our eyes, which are the most curiously contrived instruments. In their appreciation of architecture they move over it from one side to another, up and down it, away from and towards it, and all this with varying, unmathematical and altogether unprecise attention. Because of this, only the broadest of measurements could possibly register on a single façade seen from the optimum focus of the normal eye. When architecture complicates itself in three dimensions the success of any system of regulating proportions by exact mathematics recedes, revealing the essential difference between objective reasoning and the subjective intuition of design.

We are brought once again, in the face of the practical opposition of science and art in their differing approach, to a problem of creation. Yet, even so, the inference of number is there to puzzle and confound us. It is there, and it is the hope of purely reasonable men that it should be separated out and made the subject of scientific study so that, once knowing the mathematical basis of art, we might refine our senses by using this knowledge at the very moment or period of otherwise intuitive creation.

A few years ago I made a design for a Teacher Training College at Wudil in North Nigeria, using in its planning a series of related

* *The Modulor*, le Corbusier, Faber, 1954.

squares, and I mention it because the idea of using squares in this way came from the pregnant feeling that this group of buildings, standing in the dusty heat of the plain, should be an enclosure gathered round a source of water and turning inward to its shaded courtyards from the unfriendly waste, and that this was to be its first act of education. Thus the ideas of enclosures symbolised by squares haunted me early in the design and pursued me through the period of intuition.

It was one which could be externalised by means of the normal drawing instruments of T-square and 45° set-square with the minimum of interference with the progress of the design, and it seemed a virtue that it had arisen from the emotional state in which the design had been conceived (plate 13). I doubt whether I could have managed anything more complicated, but I am sure that the design benefited from its intervention.

I remain unconvinced of the efficiency of le Corbusier's Modulor as a tool that I personally could use. In his hands it is a chariot to heaven; but in others it can be a bus to a dusty terminus. I have tried to read the Modulor book, and though it filled me with admiration for what it sets out to do I cannot follow it. Still less a pedant like Ghyka, and not even the more reasoning Borissavlievitch* who, so acute in pointing out the difference between objective mathematics and subjective design and the difficulty therefore of evolving working systems of arithmetical control over architectures, goes on to elaborate Laws of Similarity and Sameness as unworkable as the theories he has demolished.

It comes to this; that there are shapes and relationships to which the good architect aspires and in the rush and fever of creation often reaches intuitively. If they could be reached in a cooler state they would be equally beautiful, but only the rarest spirits, and by no means all of them, can or will permit the intervention of a regulator in the process of three-dimensional creation of which the animal element supplies so much of the generative force. Beauty is infinitely

Expositors of systems of mathematical proportions, M. Borissavlievitch Tiranti, 1958.

variable and is not to be trapped. It may be apprehended, and to this end the search for good proportions and the means, even the doubtfully successful means of achieving them, is the true path of the dedicated architect.

This module that has diverted us from our subject matter is in the end but a unit of measurement, a piece of building. Repeated, it is lifeless and boring, but without variety there is no rhythm. And rhythm is life, which gives point to Rodney Thomas's research into the possibilities of freedom of dimension about the vital joint between modules; how indeed to satisfy the two incompatibles of industry and art, how to find the means of importing to the reasonable and objective system of industrial reproduction the irrational, but life-giving variety and contrast of art.

I am nearly at an end of describing this final period of architectural creation, with divergences into fields concerning refinements both of art and technique.

It is to be noted, as is so often overlooked, that though it is utterly commanded by art, this workshop of the architect is conducting a business that directs the spending of large sums of money, millions of pounds of materials and structure locked up into building, so that every minute it is decided how money may be spent to best advantage. And its directions are given in the form of hundreds of drawings that descend to a detail comparable only with mechanical engineering, directing with exactitude a hierarchy of technicians for the value of whose activity the architect is directly responsible in law.

It would be better if such exactitude could be dispensed with, but it is a function of the infinite division of labour upon which the technocratic world depends, and its existence makes technocrats of us architects without bestowing any credit. But in fact technique is much less exacting than art because it is less comprehensive. The engineer who tells me that I must have eight air changes in a certain room knows little of the struggle to preserve a humanised interior, and must either go away with a flea in his ear or widen his horizons; and for lack of this humanising contact with architects, who have some understanding of technique, structural engineering in this country became mechanical and stupid.

This now-completed process of architectural creation, so incompletely described so various it is, can be taken as an example of the intuitive system at work in the world we know.

It is a most imperfect system as it stands and largely because of this it is opposed by another and more powerful system that appears to give more immediately appraisable results. But our chief concern now is with the social effects of industrialism, and we need an instrument for conducting the powers of industry towards fruitfulness. Without this they will kill us in the end; but with it we may do more than survive: we may flourish.

3 The emotional basis of architecture

Although there is in every art a rational and an irrational component, the rational component in architecture gives rise to a quantity of business so large as often to obscure the underlying artistic nature of the process; and this was never more evident than at this time. But measured in terms of the quality of what results from the creative process of architecture, the rational is dwarfed by the irrational, or to speak more positively, by the emotional side of it.

The intellect is obviously involved in the organisation and clarification of problems that precede the creative period. The architect must first be given his brief and must select the means of carrying it out with men, materials, structures, time and money; just as the painter must lay out his palette, and the sculptor weigh up his materials with the eye of a workman.

Yet even in this period the intellect, so far from being a calm, computerlike instrument of reason, is already suffused by an emotion diverting it in a direction based neither upon reason nor logic, and coloured by feelings arising from the set of facts under its review.

At this stage the subject matter is fragmented and chaotic. It is material without measure, order or direction, coming forward in all shapes and sizes, intensities and pressures. It can be given a preliminary ordering, which is in fact the brief as we know it; it may contain the materials of a system; but both the brief and the system are limited by a lack of knowledge of the range of possibilities open to them. There are, of course, briefs for buildings such as schools, office buildings and the like that, recurring with similar demands, come forward in a pre-digested state, tempting the architect to a nearly exact repetition of what is known and expected, and invoking a diminishing measure of emotional response; until finally, as in so much new commercial building in London, design degenerates into a lifeless formula giving rise to feelings of disgust and despair instead of the hope and delight that it is their purpose to generate.

Instead, therefore, of pressing on to a detailed analysis; rather than attempt the logical deduction from all the facts that could be seen to present themselves, or could be brought in, or extrapolated from, as we like to say nowadays; rather than push to unpredictable limits a rational deduction of this quite respectable order, the architect must do the reverse, or must indeed do both the one and the other at the same time, for this is not a simple function I am describing. As Anton Ehrensweig said:*

> Any work of art functions like another person, having independent life of its own. An excessive wish to control it prevents the development of a passive watchfulness towards the work in progress that is needed for scanning half-consciously its still scattered and fragmented structure . . . The artist (architect) must be capable of tolerating this fragmented state without undue persecutory anxiety, and bring his powers of unconscious scanning to bear in order to integrate the total structure through the countless unconscious cross-ties that bind every element of the work to every other element.

This, then, is a critical period in the process, because the architect, though he is committed to the solution of practical problems for social needs, is anxious to wrestle with his creative demon for the mastery of a less worldly solution. Yet if he is tempted too early to

* *The Hidden Order of Art*, Anton Ehrensweig, Weidenfeld and Nicolson, 1967.

the field his success is in jeopardy by just that departure from the basic facts upon which his solution must be based. These facts are drawn from the life-stream and will minister to it at a later stage, and if neglected or over-manipulated the solution suffers by a loss of veracity, which is one of the moral components of art.

Architecture, like all art, is purposeful, and not only in its obviously practical but in its aesthetic aspects. Alvar Aalto was once asked to design a *jardin inutile* in Paris. 'Can you imagine such a thing?' he said, 'Can you imagine anything useless?'

But the real use of architecture considered aesthetically is not at all obvious. It is ultimately concerned with the need to establish ourselves as purposeful entities in defiance of the dissolving effects of time, and it aims at significance. If we were to say that its purpose is to attach us to life so that we find life significant, and wish it to continue, we might be near the mark. And it would mean also that architecture, like all good art, is essentially hopeful and could be neither negative nor truly abstract.

The continuousness of life leads naturally towards dissolution. It breaks down into endlessly hurrying atoms; its normal tendency is to revert to sameness; towards a state of unidentified chaos.

But in its course it has produced us, and we, as endlessly perhaps, seek to find meaning in the chaos and to identify ourselves with the idea of a meaning. We interrupt this flux of events to create, in varying states of the temporary or the permanent, however you wish to put it, the forms of society that gather round ideas; and, lest they should too quickly vanish, we enclose them in caskets of art and in religion, poetry, sculpture, painting and architecture; in whatever has, for longer or shorter periods of time, form and significance.

Architecture is therefore a form that encloses a human activity which it transcends in serving the reality that brought this activity about. One aspect of its truth lies in the fidelity with which it serves its present purposes; the other rests upon the intensity with which its author experiences life and seeks its meaning.

Thus every building is unique and anticipates the future, and the power it exercises over us lies in its deep attachment to a range of human emotions from the animal to what the Romantics called 'the sublime'.

I used to imagine that architecture could be explained in terms of what we see, which is indeed the normal practice, until one day I had to account for the excessive emotion, the wailing and the wringing of hands that greeted my early examples of modern architecture in this country. And I saw that this perturbation had little to do with art but was the instinctive reaction to a sudden change in the known environment, and that if the parson of the village in which my flat-roofed house was to go up was outraged, so too was his dog likely to be, since the emotion was more animal than intellectual and could be shared by them both, and exhibited in much the same way.

Watch an animal inspecting a new set of surroundings; the domesticated dog or the less domesticated cat. With what care does it satisfy itself on all matters concerned with security, the entrances and exits, the dark and enigmatic corners, the objects in space. How alert are its senses for these inanimate things; how doubly alert, the fur rising, the teeth bared, the claws unsheathed, for what moves and has life, for what is patently animal. Then watch it reassured curled up for what passes for sleep yet is so ready for action, and ask how fundamentally we differ, how much lies apparently dormant, and what has been disguised and meticulously transmuted by our need to create, and in the course of time to complicate beyond measure, a structure of society that shall appear to us as rational, as being the only sensible and orderly way of conducting our lives.

The making of any sort of a society involves us in disguising or subduing the animal instincts that tell us to question all strangers, to have our weapons ready, to prefer a wall to our backs, and to safeguard ourselves in our defenceless moments; and in this we have recourse to art which in the form of epics and images, symbols and rituals, creates moral and ethical worlds that tell us what to do, and buttress the practical means of enforcing it. Thus law would be an ineffective code of pains and penalties lacking the moral sanction of an emotionalised morality encased in art, and if the Bible were deprived of its poetry and reduced to a rational statement of historic fact concerning human conduct it would become powerless to act as the great stabiliser that it has for so long been.

Therefore I say with a new emphasis that the emotional component of architecture is greater than the rational. Even more, that architecture seldom strays far from its animal base, for which we should be grateful.

Architecture is concerned with weight, mass, space, variety, contrast and rhythm which you would not expect to be capable of arousing such emotions, yet I still make the point that the emotional preponderates both in the creative process and in the responses it evokes, and that these range from a sense of fear, doubt, or danger to that of exaltation or sublimity.

Let us make an excursion.

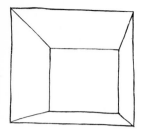

Figure 1 I have drawn the interior, three sides of a cube which I complete to show its construction, so that it becomes the sort of device used by the painter Francis Bacon to enclose his victims, though I want only to represent the appearance of the inside of an open courtyard.

Figure 2 It is but an abstraction until I set it in the world we know and give it light and shade which immediately sets up a harsh contrast; and a figure which gives it size but no real scale because its walls are blank and it could be none other than a prison, so that

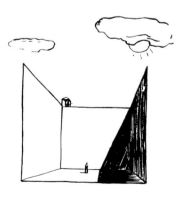

Figure 3 If I were to add a fragile sentry-box on the corner the European conscience would be stirred to memories of fear and shame.

Figure 4 Let me but pierce the wall, however meanly and inconsequentially, and fear drains away to what remains of danger in passing through this low opening into whatever lies beyond, if the beyond is indeed no more than another prison!

Figure 5 But let me indicate what lies beyond in the form of what is familiar and delightful and there remains only the fear, no longer great, engendered by the low opening.

Figure 6 And finally, I humanise the cube face with the surface markings of occupation, revelations of interiors that remove the enigmatic and give assurance, and you have the little enclosed space of an Italian town that thrills the tourist by he knows not what medley of delicious sensations, though you may be as sure that when you invite people to pass from a confined space, through a low opening, into a larger space beyond that they will have experienced a series of emotions that awaken them from their normal torpor by arousing their animal instincts of self-preservation.

Figure 7 Let me examine an example that lies at hand. The Duke of York's Steps is a notable piece of urban design that has always interested and moved me. From the slightly rising approach of Waterloo Place the great column stands on the edge of nothing – a sheer drop? a slope? steps beyond? There is no indication: the situation is tinged with the enigmatic, however reassuring the distant view of Westminster can be. The assurance comes welling in up to the moment, and it is always quite a moment, when the great width of steps, a perfect Niagara of steps, opens up below, and you are *dragged* into a descent. Now we have uncovered, I think, in the use combined with the contemplation of this piece of urban design, emotions that include elements of danger and insecurity mixed with some submission to the command exercised by the majestic symmetry of the arrangement and, I confess, to a sudden moment of vertigo at the top of the steps.

Figure 8 Reverse the process and the emotions are nearly all pleasurable since everything is revealed, or nearly everything, because the horizon of the steps divides the view into what is patently below the line and what is half-glimpsed above, a promised land that turns out to be only the Athenæum and the United Services Club but is a fairyland for the uninstructed visitor. But this division of levels is a dramatic fact to come upon in our city.

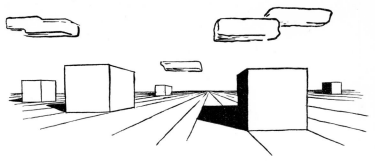

Figure 9 A further example drawn from the surrealist landscape shows a series of unidentified cubes standing on the radiating and vanishing perspective lines of a scene to a distant horizon under a sky containing some clouds, the form of which echo the shape of the cubes below. The cubes are innocent of any built-in expression, and they reveal their solidity only by the shadows they cast, but it is impossible not to feel some potency in their relationship, some sense of communication between them arising from their particular situation in space; they generate an emotion that is hard to put a name to but impossible to deny.

But in fact we are so fundamentally emotional, so charged with a vitality that searches out for us what is, or could be, significant for our continued existence and well-being, that there is no obstruction, no figure or form, no sound or sense that fails to arouse some part of our animal sensibility either to distress or to the fortification of our tenuous hold on life.

The painter de Chirico exploited in many a canvas these feelings of the enigmatic, of danger at midday, the hidden threat in the familiar scene; and other surrealist painters went on to the edge of paranoia and hallucination with every expression of suppressed or revealed sexual emotion. This motive, with or without figures, recurs at intervals and has a great deal to say to us as architects because it gives to the representation of spatial relationship a vital connection with our animal sensibilities. Its feeling of menace has been echoed in the literature of European despair from Kafka to Sartre, and, though not the emotion that architecture chooses normally to play with, it remains one that architecture touches upon before it resolves its problems in the unification of its parts.

This notion of buildings corresponding with each other in space arises more often than could be supposed in the practices of contemporary architects. The most celebrated is the Capitol group of buildings at Chandigarh where on a great plain of space le Corbusier set the four or five buildings housing the government of the Punjab (plate 15). When he first produced his layout for the Capitol group some of his closer friends thought that he had exceeded the limits within which individual buildings communicate with one another. I know that he meant to go to the limits, and that in the period when he gathered his brief and the High Court building was becoming clear to him he was constantly refreshing his impressions of those extended vistas that stretch from the Louvre to the Arc de Triomphe, of what indeed the perambulating mind can take in and resolve and find acceptable.

What le Corbusier sought after at Chandigarh was much more difficult than the grand axial arrangement of the Tuileries and the Champs Elysées, something more like the cubes in the diminishing landscape (fig. 9) since nothing in his layout is axial. The High Court and the 800-foot-long Secretariat building face one another across a plain; it is too big to be a quadrangle or a court since it covers 220 acres and is nearly half a mile across; and from it he removed all distracting movement by sinking the roads, though he added artificial hills as a later thought. On this plain between the two long rectangular buildings at each side he placed to one side the large Assembly Building, in depth the Governor's Palace (which was originally a large building), and in the space between it and the High Court his monument of the Hand, having always of course the background of the Himalayas rising 5,000 feet above the immediate background of small hills.

And that background justifies his imperious dimensions. I remember meeting a signpost at Simla that said quite simply TO THIBET, and, climbing some miles up the track to a rest house, looking out on to such a line of snow-capped mountain peaks stretching into infinity in either direction, that my mind boggled at the immensity of it but was nevertheless instructed as to the outer limits of size.

Certainly at Chandigarh the dimensions *proposed* by the background could arouse a proud architect's ambitions, especially one who, as he confessed to me at the time, was interested only in art. Well is it said that you may measure a man by what he proposes to do.

I saw the Capitol group last in a sizzling midday haze when the concrete looked at its worst, and nothing was clearly defined, which is no hour for Indian architecture. Stay for a week, enjoying the fall of the light which is the hour of Indian poetry and beauty, and this group will begin to justify itself.

On a smaller scale you will find in the view along the Piazza San Marco looking over the lagoon towards San Giorgio a combination of emotions, a collaboration with nearness and distance, the enigmatic with the revealed, the solid with the ethereal, that makes it of all places in the world the most emotionally evocative, the most magical.

Geoffrey Scott,* whose *Architecture of Humanism* first stirred this inquiry, made play with the notion of *empathy*, which the dictionary defines as the power of projecting one's personality into the object contemplated but which Scott reversed as being the feeling set up in one by what was taking place in the object. Being a confirmed Renaissance humanist he was trying to suggest that a building standing apparently on plate glass would give you a feeling of insecurity in the pit of the stomach, though in fact he was suffering, like the vicar and his dog from the shock of changing environment, and he failed to extend the spectator's reactions into the emotional world I have tried to explain to you.

What Scott would have made of the all-glass houses of Mies van der Rohe and his one-time disciple, Philip Johnson, I would be interested to know because these houses strike me as exhibiting the very

* *The Architecture of Humanism*, Geoffrey Scott, Methuen University Paperbacks, 1962.

outer limits of the assumed security of modern society, offending the animal instinct that avoids isolation and prefers a wall to the back, and standing out therefore as the intellectual fantasies they are, unlikely to satisfy the deeper needs of mankind. They exploit our intellectualised conception of security and freedom as architecture is always free to do within the limits of what can attach us to our beautiful animal base, but –

> *Tiger, tiger, burning bright*
> *In the forests of the night*

– let Blake remind us.

That you should have feelings on sight of architecture, and they not only intellectual ones, is the essence of the message, for when a court of law is exaggerated beyond life size it is to strike awe into the litigant so that he is properly overcome by the majesty of the law. And so we do for other buildings of state, using size to overawe and symmetry to define the ceremonial approach, to command the senses and exact obedience, and so on.

But if the courts of law seek to generate emotions of awe, and banks those of stability and security, there are nobler emotions associated with the deepest and most permanent human aspirations which to evoke to the full supposes a complete identification of designer with patron and subject, even more, a unanimity of purpose shared by the whole community of interests involved. At no less a concentration is it possible to think of the creative process that produced the cathedrals of the Île de France, the palaces of the Renaissance, or the temples of the Acropolis at Athens. These, the distillation of civilisations of high intensity, exalt the aspirations that lie at the core of our being and continue to do so centuries after their contemporary purposes had been fulfilled.

It is in buildings of such quality that there enters what might be imagined to be a more cerebral approach, the work of a mind rather than the mere prompting of an animal intuition. And this is so. Architecture is made up primarily of geometric shapes – cubes, cylinders, pieces of sphere, triangles and pyramids, and mixtures of all of them, figuring under the light of day or in the fabric of interiors in various states of light, but always illuminated, since form is only revealed by light.

These primary forms have each of them as much character as have the notes of the chromatic musical scale, and this derives from their effect upon our animal nature as may be observed by noting our reaction to rounded forms as opposed to concave ones, flat cubes as opposed to pointed pyramids or cones, long thin cylinders as opposed to squat flat drums. This is to consider them as static and inanimate geometric abstractions without identification or surface texture. Even so they exhibit propensities for movement or absence of movement and arouse varying degrees of emotion in us, though it would be impossible to codify their properties with any useful exactitude or to guess, still less to calculate, their effects in combination one with another. As it is they form an unwritten vocabulary of architectural feeling most of which in the normal course of events must be pieced together from the feelings set up by past experiences of architecture, regurgitated as required or kept in an emotional suspension until the occasion arises. If this awareness in an architect's life is not present, or has been subdued, his work must be barren. Without an emotional scale how can he play a tune?

The sensibility to the emotional reactions of architectural form is probably the core of an architect's creative capacity, lacking which further training adds little. Nor should his awareness be confined to architecture, but should embrace whatever exhibits form and evokes emotion: the natural scene equally with art.

This is not at all a fashionable opinion to hold these days, but I am sure that it is true of all good architects, and was abundantly true of le Corbusier, whose natural awareness was refined by a sort of methodical reflectivity. Then also in the course of his enriching experience the forms he played with assumed the added complexity of his inner life with its contradictions and ambiguities avowed.

Even so these forms are rarely used singly since architecture is a language rather than a vocabulary. They are used in combination and in series, and what is bound to be important is the relationship they bear to each other within the effect of their total combination in one building or a group of buildings considered as a work of art.

Repetition is a necessity in architectural composition, since to place expressive and emotional forms next to each other would cancel their evocative value. By the nature of things windows and supports repeat themselves in series, but if this mechanical function is all they do the fact is quickly made patent, the mind is quickly satisfied without generation of emotion.

This being the case with so much of the commercial building in the world, and reveals the extent to which business life has been mechanised and bureaucratised and has in consequence little to say to us. Even in a building as aware of itself as the American Embassy in Grosvenor Square the mechanical element, due possibly to the imposition of a mechanical diagrid structural system, deprives it of expression. Its main façade rolls out like a stamped-out metallic pattern and disappears round the corner without a nod, just as though it couldn't stop even if it would (plate 16). In this it is the true creature of its age. In other respects the building is admirable. Its base, the sturdy supports of the lower floor, the idea of a great casket resting on the base and diminished at the roof are completely acceptable, but it is the texture of the casket that fails to hold us.

The repetitive element of the new Chelsea Barracks in London starts off with the strong emotional reference to the military machine, but continuing too far is deprived of rhythm, and for this reason again fails to hold our emotions (plate 17). Repetition, to establish rhythm, must be confined by its relationship with other parts and with the whole, which is to say that it must be commanded by some sense of purpose or emotional direction that gives it life and movement.

What we separate out as architectural styles are the responses to strongly and widely held bodies of emotion concerning important aspects of life; Gothic architecture to the Christian ethic and scholastic metaphysic; Renaissance to the revived classical mythology disguising emergent materialism; and Victorian architecture, if its unselective revivalism could be seen to merit the collective title, to the need to find authentic respectability in a disintegrating world. This latter situation did not prevent men of genius, from Barry to Lutyens, excelling in the styles they adopted for their purposes, but it robbed the period of coherence; and it prevented them from knowing why they built as they did, just as it prevented them from really making free with the ornament that at appropriately lower scales supports and sustains the measure of the greater parts. Thus you will find in the close range view of buildings such as Westminster Palace or the Reform Club, a negative or static element stifling further enquiry.

I raise this particular issue because we are again in a period of emotional insecurity in which architects are pulled now this way and now that, wanting and often professing to a logical basis for their preferences, but bent by no such all-engrossing appeal to the sensibilities as made modern architects of us thirty or more years ago. We are perhaps dealing with the general lowering of all forms of expressed emotion, apart from some rage and frustration, in a society given over increasingly to mechanism and bureaucracy, and this I once found so markedly in the ceremony of cremation that I had vividly to relive the process in order to re-discover something of the true nature of the funeral rite; what constituted the due celebration of death, and what was obscuring the human necessity to share grief.

It is worthwhile examining this problem in some detail because the design of crematoria in England is evidence of a diminished sensibility in a society so compartmentalised and bureaucratised, and so misled and bemused by commercial pabulum as to have lost interest in and failed to see the significance of one of the major dramas of our existence, the death and burial of individuals. Spurning the solemnity of obsequies and turning from the proper celebration of grief, as it turns from the social responsibilities of much else that might upset

15 Photograph of the model of
the Capitol group, Chandigarh,
by le Corbusier, showing the
asymmetrical disposition of
monumental buildings on a
plain. The Secretariat, in the
foreground, and the Assembly
Building face the High Court in
the distance, with the then
Governor's Palace linking them
across space.

16 The American Embassy,
Grosvenor Square, London, by
Eero Saarinen, architect.
'The main façade rolls out like a
repeated carpet pattern and
disappears round the corner
without a nod. . . .'

17 Chelsea Barracks, London,
by Tripe & Wakeham, architects.
An example of the military
emotion over-emphasised by the
machine idea.

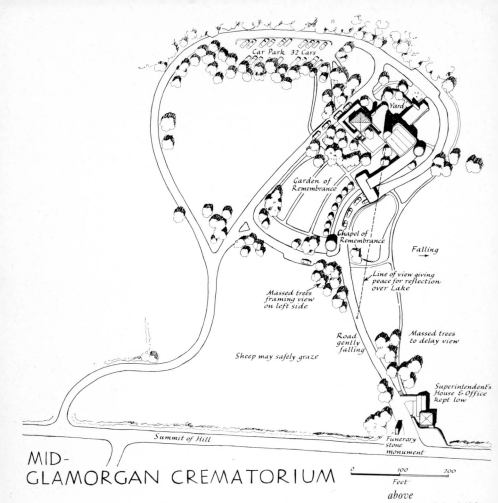

Car Park 32 Cars

Yard

Garden of
Remembrance

Chapel of
Remembrance

Falling

*Line of view giving
peace for reflection
over Lake*

*Massed trees
framing view
on left side*

*Road
gently
falling*

*Massed trees
to delay view*

Sheep may safely graze

*Superintendent's
House & Office
kept low*

Summit of Hill

*Funerary
stone
monument*

MID-
GLAMORGAN CREMATORIUM

0   100   200
Feet

above
18 Plan of the Mid-
Glamorgan Crematori
South Wales, by the
author.

19 Photograph of the
model of the Mid-
Glamorgan Crematori
taken from the approa
road. The main chape
of reinforced concrete
with supporting form
local stone. The small
chapel is in wood wit
copper roof.

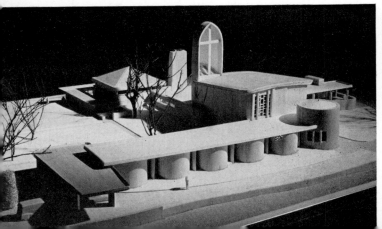

its enjoyment of the good things it has wrung from its mastery of matter, this society is as much at a loss to explain the growing volume of its useless neuroses as it was to take any effective action to prevent the wholesale murder of Jews and stateless souls, though this ranks as the greatest crime in history. Nor does it even now have any vivid sense of the connection between the two; of the approaching limits of a rational interpretation and enactment of what concerns society.

Thus with the transition from the churchyard of Gray's *Elegy* to the mile-wide cemeteries of the industrialising cities (and from this acknowledged state of overcrowding, of land hunger failing to cope with extended earth burial, to the inevitably compacted process of cremation) the transformation of a religious ceremony of moving directness and obvious significance into first a commercial and then a municipal office passed unnoticed by society. Only gradually in voicing its complaints about coffins jerking into hopper-mouth openings to the sound of mechanised music, did society come to sense some deficiency in the arrangement, yet still remained unaware of what might constitute the full cycle of its ceremony.

Reviewing the crematoria built in Europe, and they are many, I found few in which the fundamental necessities of mourning were acknowledged. There is a famous crematorium in Stockholm by the architect Asplund in which the emotional response is immediately evoked by the conjugation, at a point of the sky-line on the approach, of a cross and a funerary portal, but few others.

Good architecture of any period acts as a regenerator in setting up new impulses that have thereafter an independent existence under new circumstances. Asplund, a respecter of the past, was a born transmitter, so that long ago he told me nearly the full story of the cycle of cremation in this early announcement of sympathetic recognition. And it is interesting to note that an architect as versatile as he, one of the earliest and strongest exponents of the modern style in Europe, should be so deeply affected by the work of Sir John Soane in England. 'Why do you come to see my work in Sweden,' he said, 'when you have what you need at home?'

It was a group of small rural authorities in South Wales* that offered to set in motion the views I had advanced to the Cremation Society in 1965, and bought a site near the crest of a hill, but dipping away into a valley on one side, the background a wood with low hills in the distance. A slight shelf of land was the obvious site for the building and this, lying some distance into the land, became contributory to the essence of the scheme which is *delay* (plates 18 and 19).

What I found elsewhere to be the impediments to the act of mourning were abruptness, obviousness, peremptoriness and banality. What mourning requires is first of all dissociation from the busy, heedless life of the streets the cortège must pass through, followed by a sympathetic ceremony, all surroundings, forms and concerted actions conspiring to revive, receive, and finally to compose private grief by dignifying it in association with the past history of life and death in the region, and thereby joining the crematorium to the history and life of the churches and chapels equally with that of a secular life. I could see no point in separating them.

And for this reason, and because any degree of falseness or equivocation, such as the temporary removal of crosses or other tell-tale symbols like the reproduction of religious-seeming music, is more destructive of feeling than architectural ineptitude, I designed a chapel, with organ, for Christian worship, and a second chapel for others, each with its own road access, and each with its appropriately extended ceremonial approach. In this I was prompted by the memory of the funeral of one of our staff at Chandigarh. The body, wrapped simply in white cerements, was carried to the pyre by the river on a litter by six mourners. As the procession went forward I noticed that a man would leave it to tap one of the bearers on the shoulder and silently take his place; I did likewise and felt the burden in my turn.

So it seemed that what at least was lacking with us was our dissociation from the ceremony, and our non-involvement with grief,

* The Bridgend, Ogmore and Garw, and Porthcawl Urban District Councils and the Pen-y-bont Rural District Council.

which explains the approach cloister, with its semi-circular recesses encrusted with the memoria of past mourners, beating out a slow and comforting rhythm up the gradual slope to where the officiating priest of whatever denomination awaits the procession to lead the last few steps, still upward,* to the catafalque in its semi-circular receiving niche, lit from above. At the entrance canopy the procession, more private but no less ceremonial, must once again take up its load, and thereafter every step becomes significant within and without in forms arising from it – the halting canopy, the cloister rhythm resolved by the larger vestry drum, the ladder window marking the turn to the last few steps, and from the low ceiling of the cloister to the height of the chapel, and the niche of the catafalque carried up above the chapel roof announcing from the distance the end of the sad journey of this Christian committal. Thus also stand the stone pylon at the entrance, silhouetted against the crown of the road, the tree-planting delaying the view until it comes reflected in the calm waters of a small lake, and the – as it were – sub-dominant rhythm of yew trees leading to the isolated chapel of remembrance.

I have called this an anatomy of mourning in order to draw the attention to what some personal reflection will confirm, namely that however much we gloss over or otherwise dismiss them from our consciousness, the fact of death and the necessity for the full expiation of grief as a communal act must be freely admitted for the good of our soul and the health of our spirit, as Geoffrey Gorer has made plain enough in his documented study of grief.†

A good deal of what I have described as forming the directing impulse for the design of this crematorium was absorbed into the unwritten programme of buildings in periods in which the artist was a more important figure than he is for us at present, and the unwritten programme supposes a degree of understanding as between client and architect, even more than this, the need for the client of

* The whole chapel is slightly inclined towards the catafalque.
† *Death Grief and Mourning in Contemporary Britain*, Geoffrey Gorer, The Cresset Press, 1965.

what the architect may be supposed to provide. 'If you want a stylish architecture,' said old Berlage, 'you must live stylishly.'

The study of the human eye by R. L. Gregory* comes as an interesting footnote to this chapter. Buildings do not normally move, except windmills, and few can be seen at a glance. The human eye explores them as it does a painting, and the order in which it does so depends upon the configuration of the building.

Now, while the outer part of the eye is a rotating mechanism of the greatest delicacy dissociated from the blood stream and existing in its own fluid, the retina, so far from being a cinema screen, is a complicated nervous system that transmits messages to the mind; nor are these messages the photoprint of what comes through the lens, but far otherwise.

The photograph is the exact register of what is seen by the lens, but the retina transmits with the image of the lens the corrections that enable us to come more closely to terms with what we see, because we do not by habit look out of our eyes passively but as creatures equipped to survive: to judge distances therefore, to calculate weight and mass, to distinguish between fixed and moving things for our own good, etc.

Compared with the eye of a frog, which appears to be capable of signalling only a few things concerned with movement and corners, though responding to the presence of flies, our eyes 'are general purpose instruments for feeding the brain with *comparatively* undoctored information, while the eyes of animals possessing simpler brains are more elaborate, for they filter the information which is not essential to their survival, or usable by a simpler brain. It is this freedom to make new inferences from sensory data which allows us to discover and see so much more than other animals. The large brains of mammals, and particularly humans, allow past experience and anticipation of the future to play a large part in augmenting sensory information, so that we do not perceive the world merely from the sensory information available at any given time, but rather

* *Eye and Brain: the Psychology of Seeing*, R. L. Gregory, World University Library.

we use this information to test hypotheses of what lies before us. Perception becomes a matter of suggesting and testing hypotheses.

From what we see here of the workings of our eyes, and from the little we know of the vast unconscious world of which our recognisable life is but partly a reflection, we may guess at the difference between minds stimulated to the exercise of the faculties upon which the continued existence of society depends, and those not.

This suggests to me that it is the *quality of the emotions entertained by society* that enable it to plot and follow a course towards successful, though always temporary, survival, and that this is doubly true where circumstances, as in our Western world, are not only complicated in themselves but are over-laden with historical references and precedents. It is in such circumstances that hypotheses multiply, and the means of testing them must come to rely more and more upon the understanding of what kind of emotion we are able to summon. We find ourselves being hurried along in the midst of too many seeming events and too much information, and we are losing the power of reflection that would tell us what is important and what not.

We stand every day more in need of the type of mind capable of comprehensive rather than particular reflection, and on no subject more urgently than this question of how we are to live on our diminishing piece of earth. This is why I attempt to enlarge your appreciation of the scope of this particular art I follow, hoping that you will help to create the climate of consenting opinion in which reflection will be possible.

Though we have extended our specialised knowledge of the world in a way that could make us feel proud of what our brains and senses have done for us, yet in the doing we may feel, as I think we do, that the form of society over the period has become increasingly misshapen – all intellect and no guts, or all belly and no mind – but in either case, off all proper course and reckoning. For there are two aspects of this matter; the one an extension of our faculties, in tune with the fashionably expanding universe; and the other Blake's kind of world: 'a world in a grain of sand', and there is this finally to be said of architecture before I close the chapter: that being concerned with rhythms at the heart of which we find numbers, it is, as in Blake's lovely aphorism, directly connected with and has to speak to us of the spirit that keeps the stars on their courses.

There are, it is true, but a few buildings that exemplify this statement, but these, rising above all normal comfort levels of allusion and anecdotage and all the easier displays of emotions by which we are nevertheless deeply stirred, seem to be concerned only with the loftiest conception of ideal proportions, aiming, as in the Parthenon, at a degree of solidity and permanence by means that grosser ages discard because the intellectual tensions of a very high class of society have been destroyed by a conqueror. Occasionally it may happen in the mere fragment of a work, as, coming unprepared into the nave of St Mary's, Bury St Edmunds, I found myself in the presence of an arcade so immaculate in its proportions as to make me think it more than the work of man.

4 The age we live in

We were all born into the industrial age and are its conditioned subjects. Equally we were born into the remnants of an earlier age; into its architecture, its art and literature, and even into a lively memory of its habits of thought and manners, carried onward to us by the dwindling impulse of the time lag, kept that much alive by the art and literature we inherit.

I was born just before the turn of the century in Liverpool, and in a formative period lived in the classical inner area where a series of connected squares and terraces, not yet invaded by motor traffic, provided me with a coherent background of well-mannered order.

I might have been born into the larger area of classical inner London and been that much further steeped in the continuous historic stream connecting the eighteenth century with this. But indeed so much that has since been destroyed of Park Lane, Regent Street and Piccadilly was to be admired in the early twenties when I first came to London that I too could feel, and record, the sense of a quality of wholeness in the composition of the urban environment that has passed away; a wholeness that it is now the conscious aim of architects to re-create. This sense would have been harder to come by had I been born in Wolverhampton or Leeds; harder but not impossible, because the relics of earlier periods were widespread, and industrial England tended to gather round old centres.

Being born into this age, how do we erect personal standards? And how do we come by a critical apparatus with which to measure and judge it? As I ask these questions I marvel at the immensity of our personal background of experience, that store of memories which in the course of time can no longer distinguish between what actually happened to us and what we got from books and pictures, and which by some personal chemistry we transform into an attitude and a morality, and that particular feeling for the history of our race that appears to us to be our personal concern.

There is somewhere in the growing child a critical faculty at work selecting for him what he needs, and guiding him to experience, however apparently unselective, that will nourish the power to discriminate and to act when prompted by the occasion. This would appear to operate in circumstances as difficult as those in which young poets of the Soviet Union find themselves, a situation once vividly described by Pasternak, and now so grimly re-enacted. These young poets, who offer themselves in those harsh courts of correction as sacrifices not so much for the freedom but for the dignity of the individual, are doing our work for us.

I believe that we have come to a time when doctrines that have been held for truths, and explanations that satisfied, must yield place to what will be found more in accordance with the changing circumstances with which we must inevitably make a successful composition. What we will eventually resolve is beyond my present purposes. The best I can do is to offer what evidence I can bring forward in favour of a new appreciation of these circumstances, and to trace, as I hope to in this chapter, the rise, exfoliation and gradual hardening of a view of life which, though now questioned upon every hand, maintains its hold upon the ruling seats of power, the interlocking hegemony of industry and state.

We must therefore retrace our steps to that period prepared for by the Reformation, when it rejected the warm heart of Catholicism

leaving seventeenth-century man to face his future guided only by
his reason and a new raw conscience.

Here from our vantage point of three centuries we can watch the
European inhabitants of a world opened for them by Columbus and
Galileo, searching for an explanation with which to replace the faith-
bound certainties of mediaeval scholasticism, and finding it in physics,
that is, in a material explanation of the universe based upon reason
and deduction from ascertained and measurable fact.

But before entering upon an account of what took place thereafter
let me pause to consider what I mean by the need for a reappraisal
in the seventeenth century; it also has its parallel and fresh manifestations in these our times.

In the *Seventeenth Century Background* Basil Willey says:

> A general demand for restatement or explanation seems to
> have arisen from time to time . . . Such a demand presumably
> indicates a disharmony between traditional explanations and
> current needs. It does not necessarily imply the falsehood of
> the older statement; it may merely mean that men now wish to
> live and to act according to a different formula. This is especi-
> ally evident whenever a 'Scientific' explanation replaces a
> theological one.*

It remains to be seen how evident it may be when a scientific explanation is found so wanting as to require substantial modification.

Though an active member of the modern architectural movement
of the thirties I was never an out-and-out collaborator with industry.
I had always regarded the machine as a fate rather than an opportunity, and as the post-war period unwound itself my apprehension
grew to the strength of fears as to whether collaboration was either
possible or salutary, or in any case on what terms it could be possible,
and modified by what considerations.

The period of moral degeneration as Hitler progressed towards the
declaration of the total war when we finally joined in committing

* *Seventeenth Century Background*, Basil Willey, Chatto and Windus, 1946.

ourselves to ruthless bombing; the war itself, with all the miseries suffered by non-combatants; and finally Hiroshima, brought us to a state of near terror for the future we might be preparing for ourselves, by presenting us with a picture of disintegration much further advanced than anyone could have imagined from reading the prophetic books of Aldous Huxley or George Orwell.

These facts bore evidence also of vast changes in the industry with which architecture proposed to collaborate. War and economics had drawn both sides together, to the greater gain, one could suppose, of industry than science; and for architecture the collaboration, such as it was, had dangers unforeseen.

Something in the ease with which scientific industry closed with the ruthlessness of war altered my attitude to it. With new manifestations of its success in fields of government control, shopping and entertainment, in the palpable diminution of choice in daily life, and the new and warning note of authority in the organs of mass communications, I could no longer take it on trust. And so, setting out in 1956 for a spell at Harvard, I played with the idea of exposing my views through the medium of a conversation piece, *à la* Paul Valéry, to take place between an architect, the intelligent warden of an Oxford college and an art historian, since Oxford seemed to offer me the dramatic example of a delicate organism dedicated to reflection and learning, overthrown by a simpler structure of lower quality but with great powers of quantitative expansion, and to be the more interesting for the comparative unawareness of the university body as to the true nature or virtue of a university city, or of the fate that awaited its unguarded future.

Burckhardt held that the Italian City States owed their form and quality to the power of reflection upon the nature of cities held by their leading citizens. This might have been true of Oxford up to the moment when it was possible to measure the first effects of material growth in the person of Morris expanding his garage into a factory, and to insist upon the necessary conservation of an atmosphere conducive to learning in the fabric of the Oxford of that time. I imagined the Rector saying to Mr Morris: 'Do you think, Mr Morris, now you are doing so well, that you should move to Luton, because I fear that we may not make good housemates in years to come?' But, of course, nothing of the kind happened and Oxford came in due course to be flooded by Mr Morris' employees and by the cars they made, and now with the Meadows still in jeopardy it is a sad and sorry story.

There seemed to be all sorts of good reasons why Oxford should carry the load of my moral indignation, and by the time I reached Harvard I had rapidly advanced to the point of denunciation. But I was also in deep waters, as became evident on reading what I had done to my friend Jacqueline Tyrwhitt.* 'If anyone was ready for Whitehead it is you,' she said and pressed her worn copy of *Adventures of Ideas* on me.† So a lot of my time in Harvard was spent reading him, and Henry Adams and Norbert Wiener and others, and the conversations had a long prologue added to them, but found in the end no favour with any publisher and were put away, and are mentioned now only to indicate how I came by my source material.

Since then I have tested what I drew from the works of Whitehead in conversation with a variety of friends, in constantly recurring thought on the subject, and against such books as bear upon it. I believe that his explanations of the dilemma in which we find ourselves today are acceptable and I will put them forward to the best of my abilities.

Wynwood Read's extraordinary book *The Martyrdom of Man*‡ would make a good introduction of Whitehead. It was published in 1870 at about the same time as Samuel Butler's *Erewhon*, and tells the story of civilisation in terms of epochs dominated by war, religion, and finally intellect. It is stained throughout by nineteenth century thought but it is a story of organisms, and stresses the idea of growth from one thing to another.

The story that we are concerned with deals with the rise of intellect as the dominating motive of European thought, of the type of

* Professor Jacqueline Tyrwhitt, Harvard University.
† *Adventures of Ideas*, A. N. Whitehead.   ‡ *The Martyrdom of Man*, Winwood Reade.

intellect that was new enough in the world in Francis Bacon's time, but was already fortified by the necessity for Europe to expand beyond its boundaries and enter a new phase of history to which mediaeval scholasticism could make no useful contribution.

Thus science can be seen dialectically as the necessary outcome of change, and the instrument whereby change was accelerated. Only this explains the eruption in the seventeenth century of scientific and inventive genius which, in the figure of Sir Isaac Newton, we may take as the starting point of our story since it still centres about his famous laws of nature, the success of which in the world of physics made physics the workaday philosophy of the world.

His laws concerning the properties of physical matter were arrived at by a method that abstracted from the consideration of the problem presented everything extraneous to it. Thus, when he propounded the law which states that a stone falls towards the centre of another body, such as the earth, with an acceleration proportional to the mass of that other body (e.g. the earth) and to the inverse square of the distance between the stone and the centre of mass of the other body (e.g. the earth) he invited attention to that fact and that fact only. It was a law that held good for the crude mechanics of the situation. It was a successful mechanical explanation of a physical condition at a supposed instant of time.

The type of thinking of which this law is an example has been for close on three hundred years the methodology of science, 'enabling it', as Whitehead says

> to extract from a given situation all that could have been of value to it; and provided that all situations offered to it required an answer in terms of mechanism, in terms of matter that is; of all things being explainable in terms of matter; of the world, if the world in general was to be drawn into the system, being thought of materially, then the system was successful in everything it set out to prove.

It is important to remember that by Newton's time Europe was well launched into an expanding world that strained the material economy of countries only emerging from feudalism and with but feeble systems of communication. Materialism had not as yet been given a name, but it was in the air, and any system that offered an efficient explanation of material phenomena would be doubly welcome, on its face value, and for the support it might bring to a material view of man's duties in this world.

The system had its critics from the beginning. The philosopher Thomas Taylor, who was the first English translator of Plato and the friend of Blake, Coleridge and Wordsworth, sensed its deficiencies as a thoroughgoing explanation of events, as did Bishop Berkeley. Blake was a fiery witness to the comprehensive and opposite view of life: 'a World in a grain of sand!' he sang. But it was not in any case a philosophy but a brilliant and sufficient explanation of physical events within the restricted environment necessary to the proof of the propositions entertained.

These propositions concerned simple matters lying in or near observable proof as, for instance, that force travelled in straight lines. Abstracted out of the full flux of events, these propositions together made the laws of nature that guided physics towards its dazzling achievements in the nineteenth century – to Faraday, Clerk Maxwell and Rutherford, to the domination of world thought and the nearly total eclipse of any other explanation of life.

During the course of the century the direction of science was modified by Darwin's investigations into the origins of species and by the consequent awakening of interest in organisms as distinct from mechanisms, but so overpowering was the effect of physics upon all manner of thought that a mechanistic explanation took precedence over any other, and it needed evidence in greater quantity before science could change its attitude. It needed, among other things, Einstein with his Theory of Relativity, and his destruction of the straight line theory of light that lay at the centre of Newton's laws and the materialistic explanation of life.

Whitehead, in the two series of lectures at Harvard that are the subject matter of his best read books,* attacked Newton's theories at the centre. They had already been upset by later discoveries of science, which in the interval had moved towards an organic and away from a purely mechanical explanation of events; but there was as yet no philosophic exposition of what these changes portended for society in general. He was acting, as he explained, as a critic of systems of thought in trying to put forward a philosophy that could account for the full set of facts revealed by modern science in the environment of our modern world.

I have said earlier that Newton's laws were concerned on the whole with simple observable events which were explained in terms acceptable to normal reason and capable of mechanical proof as, for instance, that a stone falls through space at a velocity proportional to its mass and the inverse square of the distance it travels.

> Where space and time are considered materially, in a world that is, of inert matter, this theory of 'simple location' must hold good; but it is the defect of the eighteenth century scientific scheme that *it provides none of the elements which compose the immediate psychological experiences of mankind.*† Nor does it provide any elementary trace of the organic unity of the whole, from which the organic unities of electrons, protons, molecules and living bodies can emerge. According to that scheme there is no reason in the nature of things why portions of material should have any physical relation to each other. Let us grant that we cannot hope to be able to discern the laws of nature to be necessary. But we can hope to see that it is necessary that there should be an order of nature. The concept of the order of nature is bound up with the concept of nature as *the locus of organisms in process of development!*

Accordingly it is impossible any longer to conceive of a stone as falling through space in the terms of the 'simple location' that justified

---

* *Science and the Modern World*, A. N. Whitehead, Cambridge University Press, 1936.
† My italics.

Newton's laws, because so much was happening at the moment described by Newton that his law, if it were to be a law, had set aside as
irrelevant for consideration. The moment itself, abstracted out of the
consideration of time, had taken over from the moment past and
must hand over to the moment to come, and but allow this element
of time and there rushes in upon our consciousness the idea of one
thing growing into another, of one thing therefore 'prehending' another, and of their being mirrored in some way, each in each. You
may see the growth of one moment into another, or you may equally
consider the moment as 'prehending' the moment past, and the stone
no longer a simple stone simply considered, but as an organism sustained by its environment, an 'enduring pattern' of events in which
is mirrored everything that makes it possible, 'a world in a grain of
sand' as Blake instinctively recognised.

Science has come a long way since Newton's day. For the present
theory of organic mechanism

> the evolution of laws of nature is concurrent with the evolution
> of enduring pattern. For the general state of the universe, as it
> now is, partly determines the very essence of the entities whose
> means of functioning these laws express. The general principle
> is that in a new environment there is an evolution of the old
> entities into new forms.

> This . . . organic theory of nature enables us to understand
> the chief requisites of the doctrine of evolution. The main
> work at the end of the nineteenth century was the absorption
> of this doctrine as guiding the methodology of all branches of
> science . . . the whole point of the modern doctrine is the
> evolution of the complex organisms from antecedent states of
> less complex organisms. The doctrine thus cries aloud for a
> conception of organisms as fundamental for nature. It also
> requires an underlying activity – a substantial activity – ex-
> pressing itself in individual embodiments, and evolving in
> achievements of organism. The organism is a unit of emergent

value, a real fusion of the characters of eternal objects, emerging for its own sake.

Accordingly, the key to the mechanism of evolution is the necessity for the evolution of a favourable environment, conjointly with the evolution of any specific types of enduring organisms of great permanence. *Any physical object which by its influence deteriorates its environment, commits suicide.*

The foregoing paraphrase of what will reward you in reading Whitehead at greater length serves to indicate the profound changes in the current of scientific thought and its nearness, in essence at least, to the processes of artistic creation which are the concern of architecture.

Nothing could do greater damage to our present situation than to oppose science with art, as Wordsworth did; but to see science in the environment of the modern world, and in its relation to evolving society in particular, is to apply its own methodology to our present situation, to substitute a *relative* for an intolerant use of abstractions, which is the major vice of the intellect.

Since the object of this chapter is to describe the climate of opinion in which decisions in our modern world are taken rather than to follow the course of science itself, I must go on to notice the effects on society of what took place in science, and especially in physics.

European society, as I have earlier indicated, was ready for Newton. It was in process of physical expansion; it had need of a physical explanation to justify the increasingly material character of its dominant thought. So that when that justification came in the limited realm of physics and in the form of Newton's laws, society ignored the limitations and took the laws as applicable to human conduct in general.

How this happened is beside the point. Pasternak said:

> You cannot make history,* nor can you see history any more than you can watch the grass growing. Wars and revolu-

* From *Dr Zhivago*, Boris Pasternak.

tions, Kings and Robespierres are history's agents, its yeast. But revolutions are made by fanatical men of action with one-track minds, men who are narrow-minded to the point of genius. They overthrow the old order in a few hours or days: the whole upheaval takes a few weeks or at most years, but for decades thereafter, for centuries, the spirit of narrowness which led to the upheaval is worshipped as holy.

Newton was the reverse of narrow-minded, but he must fit into Pasternak's indictment, measured as he must be against the magnitude of what took place thereafter. Even so he cannot be blamed that mankind does not so much understand as feel, or that when it thinks it understands it is more often emotionalising what falls to its purpose with all the pleasure of subconscious recognition.

What could be set beside the emphasis I place on physics is the separateness of the stages leading to the materialism of the nineteenth century. Luther, in attacking the corruption of the Church as he found it, left society with an unduly heightened sense of purely personal responsibility that tended to break it up into separate consciousnesses of an isolated nature. Newton laid undue stress on the non-human and inorganic world, and by making such a success of the deductive process lowered the value of other processes for other ends. Adam Smith helped us to slide into a market economy to the improverishment of our sense of values, and Descartes by separating the spiritual from the material words made it easier to forget the one for the other. These men, each of whom left his mark on succeeding centuries, acted in relative isolation of place and time; what connected them is perhaps no more than the emergence of a general watershed in European history.

In making as much as I have of Newton I am guilty of overloading a single figure and of attributing to science that which is not entirely proper to it. In defence I would say that although science, technology and industry are separable they now combine to produce a climate that, when compared with the pre-Reformation period, we could call scientific in the sense that technology and industry acknowledge its leadership. There was always a technology of sorts, just as industry has always existed, but the particular combination that is clearly recognisable in the early years of the last century, whatever stress is placed on its industrial component as directly affecting society, merits the general description until we are later able to be more discriminate.

Early in the nineteenth century art showed signs of impoverishment as the supporting structure of the eighteenth century gave way under the growing pressure of industrialism. By 1835, which was the year in which the profession, as distinct from the art of architecture, was put on its feet by the establishment of the Royal Institute of British Architects, architecture had capitulated to plutocracy. From then on to the thirties of this century you could pick your style of architecture as though it were pastry, which it came more and more to resemble.

How rapid was the disintegration of taste may be measured by studying the design of buildings, furniture and dress over the period between the years 1830-40. Those delicate bow-fronted houses in Park Lane, the exquisite shop fronts of old Regent Street, the Wellington tables, the gazelle-like mahogany work boxes, the finely-fashioned phaeton into which Jane Austen's prettily dressed young ladies were invited – these things did not so much disappear as become bloated, lose their finesse, and change masters as they entered the workhouse of the mid-nineteenth century.

Painting, with one or two notable exceptions, descended to the depths of representational flattery or tracked helplessly in a wilderness of revivalism, while the authentic note of poetry was sounded by Arnold in the sad but lovely lines of *Dover Beach* written in 1867:

> *The sea of faith*
> *Was once, too, at the full, and round earth's shore*
> *Lay like the folds of a bright girdle furl'd;*
> *And now I only hear*

Its melancholy, long, withdrawing roar,
Retreating to the breath
Of the night-wind down the vast edges drear
And naked shingles of the world.*

Apart from the sustained magnificence of the lines, of which I know nothing to compare, the note of deprivation, of something withdrawn from life, speaks with the anguish of a hopeless duality: it is the moan of a religious man deprived of his God.

As Arnold, so Tennyson, so Newman, so every great figure of that age felt himself at cross purposes with its environment of materialism.

If you would feel the weight of what had fallen on the land, compare the lines of Arnold with these, taken at random from the *Prelude* of Wordsworth, written between 1797 and 1805:

Dust as we are, the immortal spirit grows
Like harmony in music ; there is a dark
Inscrutable workmanship that reconciles
Discordant elements, makes them cling together
In one society. . . .

The fact is that poetry, like art, religion and philosophy, had been set aside as unnecessary to the successful promulgation of a science either in its supposedly fine and utterly sacrosanct state, or as applied to human activity as machine industrialism.

As the century advanced, science shed its early intolerance and widened to embrace ideas of process and organisation that came in to it from several directions. But Pasternak's estimate of the time lag in human affairs explains how the materialistic ideas came to be so fastened on to society as to require an upheaval of equal magnitude to free us from them.

These mechanistic ideas created their own environment in which they could thrive, and by the end of the century this environment of

* *Dover Beach*, Matthew Arnold.

a sub-population of directionless wage slaves housed in vast dormitories of mechanically conceived slums interspersed with Blake's 'dark satanic mills' constituted a problem in itself that by its mass and weight *disposed the future towards solutions depending upon mass and matter.* To the extent that Manchester influenced Engels it could be held contributory to dialectical materialism and what has followed in Russia in the shape of materialist communism. What oppressed Pasternak is little different from what oppresses us. At least the difference is political.

The scale of an environment changes the nature of what is exposed to it, and we must think now in terms of the full flood of industrialism, not only within a multiplying Europe, but in an America spreading out over a vast continent and gathered into mighty cities supported by a ruthless economy of industrial exploitation. The scale of the thing is magnificent, but it is largely quantitative. It might be truer to say that its energising quality is constantly being endangered and corrupted by the operation of a materialist economy acting quantitatively.

We have to think now of a system, which is essentially one for reproducing machine-made articles in quantity, as acting nearly independently of science, but carrying everywhere about it the marks of its origin in Newtonian physics. It contributes to a process of increasingly intensive development of the world's resources to cater for multiplying populations saved from extinction by science. Nor are these populations, numerous as they are, without hope that the prodigious productivity of the system will now, or in the near future, lead them to higher levels of existence. But this is not a foregone conclusion.*

On every hand there is cause for rejoicing, it would seem; and yet there is something wrong. There is evidence of plenty; but a lack of wholeness.

Newtonian physics prospered by confining itself to matter and force and excluding emotion. One of the most noticeable effects of

* It would appear that the highly developed countries, particularly the USA, are pulling away from the less developed.

modern life is the steady depersonalisation of state, public and social activities and the substitution of collectives – what the Americans with their so likeable cynicism call 'captive groups' – for societies. This liquidation of the personality is the leitmotiv of Dr Zhivago. It is perhaps the social disease of our time, and it is traceable to the climate engendered by early science, taken over *en bloc* by the nineteenth century as a working faith, and built into us now by the operation of a machine economy that penetrates every part of our lives.

One of the by-products of this view of life is the worship of efficiency for its own sake. Efficiency is a measurement of output related to effort. It draws its purpose and its emotion from mechanics, to which it subjugates most other considerations. It is a typical machine-minder's word foisted on to society by a machine environment. It enables executives to carry out policies with unquestioning military precision, kissing the rod that scourges them as, in the worst example known to us, when a department of the Nazi State handled day after day, with the cautious little comments and annotations normal to civil service everywhere, and a wry joke or two no doubt, the files dealing with the scientific extermination of five million Jews. The process of de-personalisation of which this is an example is the outcome of treating essentially human problems as though they were scientific experiments, industrial programmes or commercial campaigns, and, if I am right in tracing its origins to the *cast* of thought emanating from Newtonian physics, then it is maintained by the total environment of a machine economy and will be intensified, if we listen to Norbert Wiener, by the development of electronic machinery of communication.*

In a fascinating book, that on the evidence of its oddly worded title is a study of society by way of its communications, Norbert Wiener finds many similarities between machines and man, but his interest is in machines not man, and he has no real idea of what the effects of his science of cybernetics are likely to be on the evolution or the destruction of society. 'Messages,' he says, 'between man and

* *The Human Use of Human Beings*, Norbert Wiener, Anchor Books.

machines, between machines and man, and between machine and machine are destined to play an ever increasing part.' That is as far as he will go.

The early industrialists, in the gusto with which they exploited nature, left human beings out of serious account. It was, if we are disposed to be lenient, a sin of omission. But with the dawn of the new century, as the materialist religion became ingrained and growing populations offered wider fields to expanding empires of industry and government, the objectification of the individual assumed an imperative, and sense of sin vanished. It became a virtue to think of people as being material for manipulation for the purposes of big business, big government, or total war.

Throughout the whole of the process the machine can be seen at work levelling, codifying, tabulating, arranging its material in the form it can best deal with; attending first to objects, seeking standards, lowest common denominators, coefficients; perfecting itself in reproduction, eliminating friction and fatigue, and extending everywhere into new fields. But of necessity, out of the very nature of its reproductive capacity, it turns to the control of its demands, to the elimination of competition, and finally to the standardisation of demand by the narrowing of choice and the education of its consuming public through persuasion, cajolery, and intimidation.

What is permissible in a market huckster facing the customers gathered round his stall – the exaggerations, the innuendos, the downright lying that still offers to be exposed, the knowing wink, the dirty joke – becomes an impertinence and an invasion of our proper sensibility when it assumes the proportions of a national campaign.

Marghanita Laski is right, and I am with her, in detesting modern advertising and all the nefarious practices it follows under the cloak of the common good. Given the power of limitless reproduction and the immediacy of photography it is nearly impossible that advertising should reach even the threshold of art. Years ago Frank Pick of London Transport tried hard to communicate with the public in a series of posters in which modern artists, and most successfully

McKnight Kauffer, grappled with their medium of colour reproduction and charmed us with each new poster they created. Since
then the pressures have mounted and the art declined. The bombardment is now ceaseless and our senses are numbed.

Among all the 'captive groups' of which civilisation is increasingly
composed the class of advertising consultants, important agents in
this war on civilisation, are the most to be pitied, or despised. Yet
we should be warned against nominating enemies that are but the
effect of forces greater than themselves and to which we are all in
greater or lesser degree subjected, as may be seen in the example of
the national press which in my own lifetime has been transformed
as an effect of machine economy. Newspapers were once local, and
arose from the need of a community for news of what was taking
place about it and to a lesser extent in the world outside. Such newspapers purveyed the news as an obligation to the community and
offered some strictly editorial comment.

With the growth of communication and the increase in population,
demand could be met only by an increase in the speed of printing,
and the rotary press was invented. But the capital cost of the
machinery and the need to safeguard supplies of paper and pay
rising wages was beyond local resources. Amalgamation of newspapers resulted, and advertisements formed an increasing part of the
revenue, revealing (as newspapers swelled to receive them to such an
extent that a copy of the *New York Times* could be mistaken for a
bundle of what once passed for a single newspaper) the working of
a Gresham's Law of communication whereby too much turned out
the little that was. Finally, and naturally, power became concentrated
in a few so-called 'press lords' fighting, not for the standards of an
incorruptible press, but for the advertisement revenue of huge
blocks of the public, to whom the newspapers now appeal with the
blandishments of nearly undisguised entertainment, subtly insulting,
familiar, but impersonal. Who is in command there? Is it the press
lords? or the mechanism that owns them?

But whether the press is corrupt is beside the main point, which

is the universality of the influence of the machine continuously destroying the continuously renewed efforts of society to create symbols
in its own image, germinative rather than sterile.

Modern life, dominated by reproductive machinery, has become
a never-ending succession of stimuli coming to us through our eyes
and ears from newspapers, radio, television, gramophone, public
address systems, etc. It is obviously impossible to attend to them all
with equal intensity, and for a great number of them we lack either
knowledge or interest, and respond only by relegating them to a sort
of second consciousness, deadening ourselves in order to escape the
quantity of them but adjusting ourselves in the process to accept a
view of life that is fractionised, atomised you might say, and of
lessening value. 'Photography has accustomed us to its unfeeling
perception' says Erich Kähler.*

Thus, for instance, we are by modern processes of exact colour
and texture reproduction in touch with the best art the world has
produced. But now it is Cézanne, then Titian, then early Christian
art, cave paintings, African sculpture. There is no end to it, and as it
multiplies so its stimulus declines, and it ends in a row of fabulously
produced books tightly wedged into a contemporary book shelf as a
symbol of latter-day respectability. As with art, so with music, the
world's classics competing in vain with the cross talk of the sitting
room or the drone of the hoover. Only television keeps us rooted and
destroys the social sense at its nerve centres!

Sir Kenneth Clark† in a Granada Lecture spoke of the difficulty
of transmitting ideas through the medium of television due to the
necessity of simplifying the allusions upon which the exposition of
ideas depend, hampered from the start by a pervasive flattery operating upon both audience and performer that inheres in the machinery
of mass communication, and but another instance of the Gresham's
Law to which I refer in connection with the press which I. A.
Richards fears as a possible 'collapse of values'.‡

* *The Tower and the Abyss*, Erich Kähler, Jonathan Cape, 1958.
† Sir Kenneth Clark, Granada Lecture.
‡ *Principles of Literary Criticism*, I. A. Richards, Routledge & Kegan Paul, 1926.

20 Aerial view of classical Bath,
portraying the urban aspect of
the last successful civilisation in
England, upheld by a firm social
structure and served by a
system of building and transport,
the machinery of which was
fully understood.

21 Industry, railway transport and dwellings in mortal combat for ground space. No mutual understanding emerges from the competitive chaos.

22 Intersection of two 'freeways', east of Los Angeles Civic Centre, California. The freeways are magnificently free where all else is confined.

One cannot escape the realisation of a defect, an error at the core of all these reproductive instruments, making it impossible that they can be educative in the proper sense of the word, but rather the reverse, despite their evident value as entertainment, which is a sure way to the senses. The answer must lie in the impulse for their being reproductive rather than creative, the fact that in the cycle of performance there is no community. There is the activity of the machine reproduction, as in the cinema, radio and television, but this is met passively; there is no actual contact, and the cycle lacks organism and is indeed another effect of what this chapter is concerned with.

One of the impediments to wholesome criticism is the growing rigidity of over-institutional life which has created collectives of seemingly intelligent people – very intelligent within the confines of their collective – who are nevertheless unable to exercise a critical faculty of any comprehensive nature or to recognise value.

I belong to an Institution covering the profession of architecture which in the time I have been a member has built a high wall around its membership. I fought to prevent the passing of a registration act, the first effect of which was to transfer the final control of membership to a state-controlled council and to widen the breach between the half-separate profession of town planning and those of civil and structural engineering. I fought against registration because architecture is an art, and it is now clear that the situation calls for a greater degree of co-operation between architecture, planning and engineering, and that registration has made it less possible. And while I say this I am conscious of a certain temerity in dealing with what lies outside my profession. I feel the pull of professionalism.

Architecture is a less cramping profession than others, but

the dangers arising from this aspect of professionalism are great, particularly in our democratic societies. The directive force of reason is weakened. The leading intellects lack balance. They see this set of circumstances or that set, but not both sets together. The task of co-ordination is left to those who lack either the force or the character to succeed in some definite career. In short, the specialised functions of the community are performed better and more progressively, but *the general direction lacks vision*. The progressiveness in detail only adds to the danger produced by the feebleness of co-ordination . . . the novel pace of progress requires a greater force of direction if disasters are to be avoided.*

One feels this, of course, in the organisation of urban life, the state of which in all countries affords a major criticism of the system under which we live. In its detailed items of activity, in the provision of roads, pure water, sanitation, gas, electricity and so on, there is a high level of detailed performance, but in the whole there is something approaching chaos, a lack of co-ordination that results in our being permanently surrounded by dislocation and friction, a reflection of the fragmentation of life to which we are so constantly subjected in the press and nearly every form of entertainment and education.

We produce, for instance, the most elaborate and meticulously accurate ordnance survey maps of the chaotic wilderness we call towns. Aerial photography enables us to do it better and quicker. But what to do with the town only now do we begin tentatively to see, for what we can do is a reflection of our minds, and we are not yet free.

I stood a few years ago before two canvases in Melbourne Art Gallery. They were river scenes, one by Constable, the other by Turner, and as I was absorbed into them in a state of happy acceptance of what they had to say to me of harmony and goodness, I wondered what it must have been like to have lived in a pre-industrialised age. From which, with their image still in my mind, I came to the street outside, and it was as though I had been struck in the face by the discord of it, by the crazed perspective of electricity poles, the jagged discontinuous street line, the hard insensitive-

* *Science and the Modern World*, Chapter XIII, A. N. Whitehead.

ness of the immediate surfaces of road, pavement and buildings, the background of unorganised urban data.

There are worse streets in Melbourne, which is a spacious city full of the possibilities of redemption. To its citizens I would say in respect of these two canvases that they had made a true estimate – they are works of art of high quality – but in respect of the city as a whole it is not a work of art and cannot be so until its citizens come to value art above materialism, harmony above discord. As they do so it will become beautiful.

This ugliness of cities, their disharmony, offers evidence drawn from the surface of contemporary life of the diseased nature of what takes place beneath it, exemplifying the elevation of the object over its human reference and quite properly described as an aspect of materialism.

In my working life as an architect I am constantly in conflict with an insane expertise that goes for sense in fields of engineering subsidiary to architecture. There is, for instance, a so-called science of illumination that in its quest for a ridiculous ideal of over-all lighting leads us to great expense of equipment and current, in useless competition with daylight, with which it could never be compared. It aims to eliminate shadow as though it were as shameful as sex, not realising that shadow reveals form and that without contrast there is no definition or value. The world these technocrats live in has no place for value, but in the present circumstances of technocratic education it is an expanding world.

The science of acoustics will produce you a concert hall in which every note of every instrument carries clearly to the furthest seat, as in the Festival Hall in London, and still lacks resonance. In the old Queen's Hall, and in the former Philharmonic Hall in Liverpool where I heard all my early music, the construction was of brick, timber and fibrous plaster, and the architectural forms were simply rectilinear. Also, the platform on which the orchestra played was of wood keyed into the floor, the side boxes and the galleries, so that everything was continuous, and as a result the audience not only got notes coming to them off the circumambient surfaces in mathematical certitude, but sound everywhere; the whole place was filled with sound; airborne, reflected, reverberated; it shook with sound; it was like a fiddle itself, and when the double basses got going the great thrumming of them passed through the floor boards to you and you got everything.

I remember being taken round the Radiohaus at Copenhagen by its genial architect . . . and coming into a small concert hall. 'See,' he said, 'the acoustic louvres, electrically operated, that allow us to control the reverberation length for chamber music, light music, or jazz, . . . wonderful, is it not?' They were set for chamber music when the hall was completed, and so far as I know have never been altered since!* 'We Danes are not so excruciatingly sensitive as all that,' he added with a grin. But observe the cynicism.

Despite the most prominent acoustical failures we are building and will build more theatres and concert halls, widening in the process – a semi-scientific process – to include what escapes surface measurement and verges upon real value appreciation. But it must be realised how difficult it is, competing with fire and other regulations and with the preferred inorganic materials, and designing for mass audiences, to achieve conditions really favourable for music.

These examples lie on the fringe of the matter and indicate only the climate of opinion in which decisions great and small are taken, and in particular the reverence for things and mechanical facts over direct observation and a wider reference. In all this it is the misplacement of physics and the reliance upon specialised and therefore partial investigation and deduction that is at fault. The system in its incalculable productivity has raised the material level of life everywhere. Its mechanical effects are more noticeable because most of them make a noise of some sort, from the early snort and whoosh and hiss of railway locomotives to the roar of cars and the hum of

---

* I have been able in a country that did not plague me with regulations to make a legislative chamber cased in interlocking timber that provides acoustics at conversational level without recourse to any electronic aids.

dynamos. But in fields of medicine and genetics, for instance, the achievement is no less: wherever science turns its enquiring, measuring mind nature yields up its potentiality for increase. Its most dramatic conquest lies in the field of mechanical transport. For hundreds of years the rate of movement was keyed to the horse, and on macadamised roads skilfully designed coaches reached speeds of 10 to 15 miles an hour, which shocked de Quincey. Within a few years the development of steam locomotives took the speed up to 70 to 80 miles an hour, a phenomenal increase maintained for three-quarters of a century and suddenly surpassed by aircraft, the development of which under the pressure of two wars sent the graph rocketing, literally rocketing, past the barrier of sound and away to the moon.

We can leave the moon to look after itself while we notice the effects of rapid transport on the society of the earth.

Popular attention is so nearly entirely centred upon the instruments of transport – trains, ships, cars and aeroplanes – that it is next to impossible to direct attention to the whole process of which they form a part. Yet in terms of modern science they could not be said to exist without their environment, which not only makes them possible, but suitably adapted, prolongs their usefulness.

Thus, railways in England were first created to bring coal from the pits to the industry and the towns. That was the basic cycle that justified their development and enabled them to meet an expanding and more varied demand. They were, as we know, developed in a one-sided and entirely materialistic way, serving their basic purpose only by and large, and owing to lack of co-operation between rival interests, at great expense; but elsewhere destroying the beautiful structure of eighteenth century urban living as though it counted for nothing. Charing Cross railway bridge is a monument to the system: it is a brutal piece of engineering in itself; it wipes out one of the finest bends in the river Thames at one blow. It took someone as wilful as George Bernard Shaw to say a good word for it.

Railways occupy a lot of land, and their limitations as a system of transport impose a burden of large-scale works which it needs skill and artistry to reconcile with the predominantly domestic character of any city. But reconciliation was never impossible, and as steam, smoke and dirt are banished it becomes every day easier to accomplish. What made it impossible was the narrow-mindedness of railway engineers backed by the thoroughgoing materialism of the public which saw no connection between railway development and the creation of a balanced and enjoyable urban life.

The eighteenth century has achieved this state in what we have assumed to have been the last successful civilisation we know of in England upheld by a firm social structure with leadership, and served but not dominated by systems of building and transport the machinery of which was fully understood.

By comparison with this civilisation, the cycle of which railways formed a part was dislocated wherever it came into contact with social and urban structure, and can never be seen to have functioned with any great degree of harmony. In countries which developed their railways at later dates than England, and where, as in Switzerland, they were early electrified, the reconciliation between the single form of transport and the body of the towns was more complete, and it is noticeable that these countries have been able to improve upon and modify their systems and their city terminals with greater ease than we have.

The case of the motor car is parallel with that of the railways. Once again public attention is focused on the car itself, to the neglect of the whole process or cycle of which the car is a part. Just as we built tube railways out of London without a thought for their planning potentialities in terms of new communities settled onto agricultural land; just as we left all that to fend for itself at the hands of whatever competitive forces it generated, so we let loose an expanding mass of motor cars on the roads of town and country and only gradually saw the connection between the two, but still see little enough connection between the car as an agent of rapid transport and the idea of a desirable life in either cities or country. The first effects of popular motoring were to increase and flatten out the spread of cities, which are what might be expected. Suburbs gathered round railway stations; the ubiquitous car spread the load.

This phenomenon is to be seen in the United States on a scale that dwarfs any idea of social community. The automobile suburbs of Detroit, which I once traversed in search of Mr Saarinen, was a region of hundreds of square miles in extent uniformly exploited for a uniform population of technocrats, inhabiting houses uniformally distributed over a flat landscape in undifferentiated boredom, but seared across with masterful highways lined with advertisements. It was a formless chaos adding up to nothing, repeated everywhere in the States, and reaching its apogee in the endless city regions of California.

Now, upon this undifferentiated pattern of human occupation – what more could one call it? – the emerging engineer structure of road transport is imposed in the form of mighty car-ways, sunk into, or more normally elevated above, the ground in designs beautiful in themselves as responding affectionately to the demands of fast-moving cars, but utterly out of scale with any conceivable communities on the ground, and leaving the individual out of account entirely. The charge upon the community in terms of money is prodigious, but the other charges are yet to be assessed.

The picture before the eye of the honest traveller unembarrassed by predilections for technocracy – and I like to fancy myself as being in the company of Henry Adams of Boston for the pleasure of it and as some measure of protection from the more rabid upholders of the American way of life – the picture presented by the facts of the landscape is composed of a uniform pattern of human occupation on the ground, uninteresting because undifferentiated; and a gigantic, forcefully imposing, and in itself often beautiful structure, straddling the pattern between distant reference points of juncture with the ground and overawing it completely.

Here one glimpses something more of the true cycle of the motor car; but not enough, for having achieved the uniform spread of human occupation and the canalisation of traffic which the nature of the vehicle inexorably demands, the mighty flow is decanted back into the pattern, and between the rat-race of the highway, the pile-up into the city, and the social stagnation of the suburb, it might be guessed by as unperturbable an outsider as Adams that man himself was not in control of the affair. That would appear to be the admission of the planning authorities of New York City with its over-dense occupation of the land, its overloaded subways, bankrupted railway and the over-emphatic highway structure serving so small a part of the daily respiration of its working population. It may as clearly be inferred from the gargantuan structure of Kenzo Tange's plan for greater Tokyo.

Everywhere in the world we begin to realise the presence of ceilings to human expansion, and perhaps far from this being the explosive age to which the newspapers are so fond of referring, it may be the beginnings of a containment in which it can at last find the form it should assume. Its activities are most certainly explosive but the explosiveness is one-sided and more spasmodic than formerly. At Cape Kennedy, America spends its treasure in a space race against Russia to the moon while New York for the first time in its history runs out of water. The populations of Europe edge up towards levels of American productivity and affluence while half the world, swollen in useless numbers by applied science, faces starvation.

The most obvious ceiling, and one to which society is most loath to give its attention, is our capacity to sustain the motor car to which I have just referred. This you will find written large in the only work on the subject that even entertained the problem of values as being set beside expediency, expansion and old-fashioned ideas of progress.

Colin Buchanan's *Traffic in Towns* attempts to define a ceiling for car-ownership in Britain by defining salutory environmental standards, but this done, and the diminished flow applied to a selection of towns, large, small, historic and highly concentrated, the results are still anti-social, astronomically expensive and generally unrealisable. His application of road-engineering principles that were a prominent feature of his report were applied to Liverpool by Mr Graham Shankland to what I can only consider to be the overthrow of what civic coherence remained after the disastrous bombardment of the last war.

The city, expanding from its eighteenth-century nucleus based on Pitt Street, had never successfully negotiated the sandstone escarpment stretching from Everton to the Huskisson area by the cathedral. It was the sort of situation that called for an open band to mark the division of interests between commercial and administrative and residential activities, but in fact expansion, except for a thinnish wedge of early nineteenth-century work, was general and undifferentiated, the escarpment saving it from the final indignity by driving the principal railway to the heroic undertaking of the Lime Street cut and tunnel, done through solid rock throughout.

Now the division of the city is to be effected by giant highways, elevated in great part and passing through it to distant regional destinations, all issuing from the mouth of the Mersey Tunnel; and this, I maintain, is not what a city is for, though it may quite logically be what we have brought it to.

But to speak of ceilings as being present even is regarded as being dangerously defeatist, and there arises an attitude of mind that would appear to me to be, unconsciously or not, taking shelter behind a crazy barricade of second-hand science against the onslaught of reality. It is a curious phenomenon, which haunts the fringes of my own profession but is sufficiently widespread to constitute a seemingly formless, though formidable, body of opinion which is directed by the hope that a logic may be found to pierce to the heart of the creative process, unseating the intuitive artist in his arrogance, and freeing the temple for the enjoyment of the reasonable man.

It is the same order of hope that sees the computer as taking over from man, and it has among the general public a support that would appear nearly incomprehensible in face of the facts were it not typical of the kind of thought by which mass opinion is swayed. If the traditional sentiment whispered: 'To live is to feel oneself limited, and therefore to have to count with that which limits us';* the newest voice shouts: 'To live is to meet with no limitation whatever and consequently to abandon oneself calmly to oneself, and practically nothing is impossible, nothing is dangerous, and in principle nobody is superior to anybody.'

I. A. Richards, in *Principles of Literary Criticism*,† speaks of the need for 'a defensible position for those who believe that the arts are of value'. Only a general theory of value which will show the place and function of the arts in the whole system of values will provide such a stronghold. At the same time we need weapons with which to repel and overthrow misconceptions, for with the increase of population the problem presented by the gulf between what is preferred by the majority and what is accepted as excellent by the most qualified opinion has become infinitely more serious and appears likely to become threatening in the near future. For many reasons standards are much more in need of defence than they used to be. It is perhaps premature to envisage a collapse of values, a transvaluation by which popular taste replaces trained discrimination. Yet commercialism has done stranger things. We have not yet fathomed the more sinister potentialities of the cinema and the loudspeaker.

My dissatisfaction with C. P. Snow's offer of reconciliation between art and science arose I believe from this failure to define any such general theory of value in which both art and science could find a place and function, and this was proved to me with lamentable certainty by the ferocious attack upon Snow by F. R. Leavis.

This chapter has been tracing the rise of industrialism from its origin in seventeenth century scientific discovery as the changing climate in which architecture and planning have continuously functioned. The collapse of an integrated society, which followed swiftly on the Industrial Revolution, we have seen faithfully mirrored in a dislocated architecture, cut off from the major struc-

* *The Revolt of the Masses*, Ortega y Gasset, Allen & Unwin, 1951.
† *Principles of Literary Criticism*, I. A. Richards, Routledge, 1926.

tural arts, and these in their turn degenerating under pressure of industrialism in process of transformation and under pressure of rising population. What this transformation amounts to is perhaps the key to our situation, since what I object to in ministrations of the second-class sciences is exactly of a piece with what troubles I. A. Richards in literature. I am attacked for my arrogance in holding, however modestly, to the certainties of art in exactly the way that Leavis suspects that he and his like were being attacked by Snow. We are perhaps the victims of Gresham's Law applied to culture.

Be that as it may, there is evidence in plenty for Sir Geoffrey Vickers' warning as to the 'End of Free Fall',* never more so than in the appearance for the first time in this long history of ceilings of possible restraint.

I have not at all done with the subject, since it is necessary in succeeding chapters to trace in some detail the evolution of an art of architecture so closely associated with the complete environment that, failing a new name for it, I must leave you mentally to confer upon it the amplitude it deserves. So let me close with a quotation from a broadcast by Erich Heller in which he discussed the transformation of meaning between the original story of Dr Faustus and its later treatment at the hands of Marlowe: 'It was a stupendous revolution, glorious and absurd'. (He is referring to the Industrial Revolution.) Its glories need no recalling. They lie in state in our universities, our theatres and museums of art and science.

But the absurd consequences pursue us, alas, with keener vivacity. For we make a living, and shall make a dying, on the once-triumphant Faustian spirit, now at the stage of its degeneracy. Piccolo Faustus has taken over the world of the mind. Wherever he sees an avenue he will explore it – regardless of the triviality or the disaster to which it leads; wherever he sees the chance of a new departure, he will take it – regardless of the desolation left behind. He is so unsure of what *ought* to be known that he has come to

* 'The End of Free Fall.' Broadcast talks reported in *The Listener*, October and November, 1965.

embrace a preposterous superstition; everything that *can* be known is also *worth* knowing – including the manifestly worthless. Already we are unable to see the wood for the trees of knowledge; or the jungle either. Galley slaves of the free wind's aimless voyaging, we mistake our unrestrainable curiosity, the alarming symptom of spiritual tedium, for scientific passion. Most of which flourishes in these days as 'science', said Kierkegaard, is not science but indiscretion; and he and Nietzsche said 'that the natural science will engineer our destruction'.

> . . . There is a connection between the threat of atomic annihilation and that spiritual nothingness with which the mind of the age has been fascinated for so long, between universal suicide and Dr Faustus's newly discovered damnation: a universe which, as a philosopher who knew his science put it is 'a dull affair, merely the hurrying of material, endlessly, meaninglessly'.

'However you disguise it,' Whitehead wrote, 'this is the practical outcome of the characteristic philosophy which closed the seventeenth century' – and which may well close the twentieth, as we alas, are bound to add, with a still more practical outcome of Dr Faustus's witty enterprise to outwit the Devil by creating a Hell of his own.

5 The pre-war years

The origins of modern architecture are obscured by the massive exfoliation of nineteenth century materialism. Movements of revolt against it – the sustained denunciation of Ruskin in England, the solid achievement of the architect Sullivan in Chicago – were swept aside by a tide of animal optimism into spheres of minor influence that need the patience of a scholar to re-assess as having a bearing on our present situation.

Time and again in England the case against the system was stated with every access of imagination and eloquence, – with alternatives worked out in detail and exemplified by full-scale models, and with the support of an influential section of the population – and failed; or to the extent that it succeeded, served only to divert development from a more promising advance. It might have been thought that England, being both the seat of industrialism and of the counter-measures of social amelioration necessary to deal with the worst effects of it, might have found the means of connecting art with industry. But this was not the case.

The Victorians felt that they had effected a satisfactory fusion of the two in the Great Exhibition of 1851, but although Paxton's Crystal Palace brilliantly exposed the system of industrialised building based upon a repeated module of factory-made components, the exhibits showed how little these principles were understood. They catered for a triumphant plutocracy by ransacking the world and every period of history for models to copy, and were creatively worthless.

If England were so sunk in self-satisfaction might not the torch have passed to America, the home of rugged individualism and the clear-sighted pioneer spirit? And so, for the time when Louis Sullivan was building the Auditorium, the Carson and the Pirie Scott stores in Chicago, it seemed to be. Once again the age was given a clear exposé of the connection between architecture and industrial method in buildings that communicated the spirit of a new art in understandable terms, and rejected it. Sullivan died a poor man living on the charity of his inferior contemporaries, and America took to itself the straight Beaux Arts architectural treatment which it saw in quantity at Burnham's Chicago World's Fair and instantly liked, casting out into the prairie wilderness Sullivan's only brilliant pupil, Frank Lloyd Wright. From then on no further prophetic voices could be heard in the roar of American progress.

In England neither Ruskin nor Morris were in a position to grasp the nature or the power of what they fought against and to lead it in strength towards some harmony with the evolving circumstances. Karl Marx made a more accurate assessment out of a greater knowledge of the mechanics of industrialism, and was yet wide of the mark in essential deductions from it.

What mattered then, as it matters now, was the emotional climate of the time, and at the end of the century this climate, both in England and America, was that of a great spending age setting a price upon fine art, and making merchandise of every architectural style that could serve to draw substantial veils across the industrial origins of wealth; the age celebrated by Henry James and Arnold Bennett, the age of Cecil Rhodes, Kipling, Rockefeller and Duveen.

I am with Teilhard de Chardin in believing that great changes have to wait for a piling up of forces before they can burst the barriers of established conventions. It is, of course, fascinating to make out a chronology of advance and to see one movement as leading to another and so to a final and inevitable flowering, but I don't think it happens this way. There are spurts that subside and fade away. There are movements that get diverted and deformed. And they lack real generative power until, suddenly, there is enough combustible revolutionary material and the course becomes immediately defined.

A great deal of the preparatory work – the accumulation of structural examples, of industrialised method, of new materials – was done by engineers. They had performed great deeds in the earliest period as artist-engineers of splendid single-mindedness, but by the end of the century they were the unconsecrated high priests of a system that affected life at very many points yet failed to give it an acceptable, even a definite form. Indeed much of what they did, and they did so much, because of this lack of human purpose for which we are now in a position to account, was destructive of form.

They needed somebody like Tony Garnier, who created in 1906 the first detailed model of an industrial community, to tell them that what they were planning was capable of conforming to lines of growth harmonious with the surrounding circumstances, and was thus inherently beautiful. Garnier was among the first to suggest a form in which industrialism could flourish, a synthesis favourable both to industry and art. On the other hand, what the architects needed was something they could handle, and this was invented and developed for them as reinforced concrete by Hennebique and Coignet in the nineties, used with great daring and skill by the engineer Freyssinet and by the architect-engineer Auguste Perret, and was ready for general adaptation as the revolutionary material by the twenties. I know that when I came into the picture at the turn of the thirties it was unquestionably the material by means of which we could best express the form of the ideas that the movement had already made current in Europe. I had very little real knowledge of reinforced concrete when I came to my first modern buildings;

enough only to realise that it was the way of release and that it contained the dynamism of a new world.

This is not to say either that reinforced concrete alone made modern architecture possible or that Gropius had no antecedents. It is not to say that Sullivan in Chicago in the 1890s had not a clear view of the capacities of his art given the favourable circumstances; or that Otto Wagner in Vienna, Berlage or Van der Velde in Holland, were not the precursors of Gropius. But it has to be recorded that Burnham's idea of architecture proved to be more to the taste of Chicago than that of Sullivan's and became a deal too strongly entrenched for his disciple Wright to fight against; and that the ideas of the European exponents of modernism made small headway until really favourable circumstances found their interpreter in Walter Gropius.

Whatever were the antecedents of the modern architectural movement and whatever the later divergencies from its original form, it was born, like Pantagruel, fully fashioned in the mind of Walter Gropius, when he set up the Bauhaus as his prime instrument of realisation. He had built his celebrated Fagus Building in 1911 (plate 23), in which for good and all the industrialised wall of steel and glass was worked out, and he had carried the idea a stage further in his building for the Cologne Werkbund Exhibition in 1914. There was left for him but the time for reflection – which the First World War gave him in plenty – for him to see, to the extent that anyone at that time could see, the whole range and depth of what he was about.

The Bauhaus could be described as an industrialised arts and crafts school. What Gropius inherited from Van der Velde had more of art and craft than of any other characteristic. He industrialised it in the sense of its being set in an industrial context with a workman's ticket rather than a diploma at the end, and of its being an essentially workable experiment in what was becoming an increasingly theoretical world, as the very name implies. Looking like an elegant factory, equipped with modern machinery and tools and a design programme to put them to good use, the description falls far short either of the objectives or of the system of search and experiment through which they were achieved (plate 24).

No one else had the same intellectual grip of the situation, the real feeling for industry, the modest and single view of the idea of work, a morality so much in tune with the associated disciplines. Few of his contemporary architects thought of what the proposed fusion with industry truly implied. Walter Gropius provided the hard thinking. As Cromwell wrestled with his demon searching for his instrument of power and fashioning his Model Army, so Gropius wrestled to find at last in the Bauhaus the instrument with which to strike deep into the heart of the European canker.

> The Bauhaus was founded in 1919 with the specific object of realising a modern Architectural art which like human nature was meant to be all-embracing in its scope . . . concentrating primarily on what has now become a work of imperative urgency – averting mankind's enslavement to the machine by saving the mass-product and the home from mechanical anarchy and by restoring them to purpose, sense and life . . .*

Better still:

> What the Bauhaus preached in practice was the common citizenship of all forms of creative work, and . . . their interdependence in the modern world . . . Our ambition was to rouse the creative artist from his otherworldliness and to reintegrate him in the workaday world of realities, and, at the same time, to broaden and humanise the rigid, almost exclusively material mind of the businessman.

No one can doubt that this proposal of marriage to industry – for he had made an end of philandering in establishing the Bauhaus with its union card entrance ticket – was what Europe needed to bring together the divergent streams and restore art to a working function in the body of total European culture. He probably saw it the other

* From *The Scope of Total Architecture*, Walter Gropius, George Allen and Unwin. 1956.

way round; art giving some purpose and an honest job of work to industry, as it was possible at that time to do. For we must remember that the First World War divided two ways of life in Europe, as you may find put at great length by Thomas Mann, whom Gropius resembles in his capacity to combine breadth with detail.

Before that war Europe was still half feudal, carriage drawn, split into the 'haves' maintaining their formal dance and the 'have-nots' beginning to break it up. The British Treasury numbered perhaps 250 persons, including messengers; industry in Germany was compact, secretive, personal; advertising amateur; the press still local; population to be decimated, and in feared decline; a situation comprehensible and approachable.

And Gropius was a 'before the war' man. He had served an apprenticeship with Peter Behrens, a new man working on the inside of one of the new compact industrial groups in just the capacity that Gropius was later to extend to cover the whole field.

What I infer from this is a manageable situation capable of being permeated with a new set of ideas, and by comparison with the present one, not yet disclosing its true identity.

Nor can it be said that the Bauhaus covered the full conspectus of Gropius's vision. It concentrated primarily, as he has said, on 'saving the mass-product . . . from mechanical anarchy' by bringing the artist to the machine lathe, as it were, and rubbing his nose on it. But at the other end of the scale was town-planning, and what from the beginning moved me about Gropius was his range.

The hard, uncompromising fabric of the Bauhaus building, that I now realise to have prompted my Cromwellian image, was a rigorous exercise in industrialised method. It did not just look it. It *was* the system in process. And not far away Gropius was carrying out full-scale experiments in pre-fabricated house building on the lines now recognised to be a working rationale. But what made him finally leave the Bauhaus to continue on the impetus he had given it was the clear call to solve the larger problems of town-planning using the outlook and the methodology of the Bauhaus. In this he was one among others, but wherever he was I see him like a great serious Toscanini with his orchestra, and not without an imperious rap or two on the rostrum, curbing folly, reducing excess, and contributing to the establishment of as grand a model of a true aristocratic world of industrial order as the world has seen since.

If we are to create in the likeness of industry then we must extract from industry the virtue of its inherent order and humanise and dignify it through art. This order is not essentially complicated: it is not essentially different from kinds of order the Romans recognised; but it is an order of economy, and mainly a straight line order in which repetition is an obvious virtue. To have nurtured this virtue in terms of high architecture was the achievement of the group of architects in Weimar Germany that produced the famous *siedlungs* of Berlin, Frankfurt and elsewhere; the Bruno Tauts, Ernst Mays, Hans Scharouns and others who worked with them to lay the foundations of an absolutely workable modern architecture.

Herbert Read* noted the similarity between the great fling of these housing layouts and the small mechanisms of industry, and indeed they were of a piece in issuing from the same stable; but the similarity ends with the aerial view, that great deceiver. On the ground these fine sombre arrangements of blocks of accessible, human dwellings were invested with an art of such scale and grandeur as make most of our New Towns in England look by comparison like boyish pranks. In Peter Behrens' office at one period of time were three men who were to dominate architecture from then to now; they were Walter Gropius, Mies Van der Rohe and le Corbusier. When I first came on contact with the new architecture in Germany I was struck by two things; the first this vision of a grandly proportioned urbanism taking in everything: dwellings, roads, factories, markets, down to the small paraphernalia at the closest personal context. Here is an architecture, I said to myself, capable of everything. Here is a true resolution, the end of discord. This is it. I was swept with a fervour that was the reflection of a

* *Art in Industry*, Herbert Read.

release of creative energy which was to spread from Europe to every part of the world and change the character of architecture decisively.

Then the second thing was added to me when I fell in love with a house by Mies van der Rohe, his Turgendhat Haus, in the Taunus Mountains. I fell in love with this building, which is to say that I gave my heart to it and it entered into my emotional recesses and filled them to overflowing (plates 26 and 27).

It is very necessary that not only architects but all persons of discrimination should fall in love, and keep falling in love, with manifestations of art. It is in this way that sensibility is developed and a body of taste created, lacking which there are no points of reference for the decisions upon which the quality of life ultimately depends.

It is additionally necessary that architects should fall in love with buildings, because it is in this way that art is propagated. To reproduce art mechanically puts more people in touch with the original stimulus, and in fact I fell in love with photographs of the Turgendhat Haus. But there is a limit to what mere reproduction of works of art can do, and it is beside the present point, which is that the act of falling in love involves deeply stirring emotions that transform the lover who is thereby born again.

For me at that time it was as though, my mind cleared, rinsed, and invigorated by the noble rationality of the Bauhaus, the breadth and grandeur of the proposition that it and the Modern Movement represented to me, suddenly my heart was taken, by one work, not essentially different, but of a quality of which I had not imagined the movement as yet capable.

We talk of classical and romantic periods as though the bent of all minds together were inclined in the same direction, whereas there are at all times minds of rational, romantic or classical disposition which will minister to this element in us as it arises, but, more than that, will deal with emergent events according to the particular chemistry of their composition.

What I had found was the classicist of the movement exhibiting in this work his especial propensity for dwelling upon the type solution, for distilling out of it the virtues of the systems it represented, the essence of its communication to us of what concerns our well-being in the situation in which we find ourselves. Unlike the bulk of contemporary new work it was of steel frame construction: slender cruciform high grade steel columns sheathed in stainless steel, placed at the limits of their span and supporting a simple slab to create a space lit on three sides by plate glass windows occupying the entire space in sliding units of the optimum length. The simple two-storey structure on the side of a hill rested serenely on a stone podium approached from below by a flight of steps designed for a grave goddess to ascend, and I used to imagine her as being Frau Mendelsohn, who was as near a goddess as I had come at that time.

The interior was a creation of the utmost originality, but seemed as old as time. Nearly the entire space of the ground floor was open, divided only for the functions of the most elegant living by screens of marble or plywood, of elemental simplicity and enclosing arrangements of furniture, the rare prototypes of the modern movement disposed in patterns fixed inevitably by the mental rigours of its creator.

This was a model, complete in every detail, placed at the disposal of the ruling élite of the technocratic world – if it were so far disposed to acknowledge its power as to celebrate the fact in architecture. Its author, a man of the fewest words and the rarest appearances in the movement, later declared himself in saying 'I give you the soul of technocracy'.

There exist some studies in drawing and model form of crystalline skyscrapers, some using straight and others curved plan shapes. They had little or nothing to do with Corbusier's Ville Radieuse. They had no social message. They were the early musings of an artist in contact with technocracy, and were to be realised later in Chicago.

He permeates the period under review without again taking a principal or what would seem to be an active part in its architectural politics, meaning that he was seldom if ever present at the meeting of CIAM* where the movement consolidated its attitude and from which it extended its influence in the world.

To bring CIAM now into the narrative extends the review of the movement beyond personalities to cover the many countries whose working groups were represented at the conferences that took place from time to time.

The first of these in 1928 was at the Château of La Sarraz in Switzerland, the home of Madame de Mondrot; the most decisive and momentous on a liner cruising among the Greek Islands. They all served the purpose of bringing together, as co-workers and friends, the modern architects of Europe, principally, but of many countries of the world in later stages, to discuss the critical problems of urbanism and architecture in an industrialising world, but to discuss them as an art, and on the evidence of buildings achieved, and projects, real or hypothetical, examined.

It set itself tasks – the minimum house, the planned environment, the core of the city – and drew from its constituent groups material in the form of completed buildings, projects and serious studies of which, for instance, the English group produced the MARS plan for London, all of which served as background for discussions leading to pronouncements or publications on the various subjects.

It was a coming together of friends, its organisation sustained by goodwill and purpose, and it was pre-eminently an association of which the value lay in ideas. If it represented national groups such as the MARS group of England, then they too represented the ideas of their members. It was, therefore, supra-national, and in it a declared communist fared no better than anyone else, but rather the reverse.

Its national groups consisted generally of a few dedicated members tightly bound to each other, despite variation of temperament, by the necessities of a situation deteriorating at the onset of barbarity in Europe. The Germans were disintegrating, the Dutch

* Congrès Internationaux d'Architecture Moderne.

fiercely uncompromising, the Scandinavians politely omniscient, the Poles political, the Italians accommodating, the English willing, and the French quarrelsomeness was obliterated by the force and direction of the leader le Corbusier. Van Eesteren, the Amsterdam planner, presided like a father, and Sigfried Giedion, the author of *Mechanism take Command*, was a secretary sent by heaven to minister to an organisation so successful in what it set out to do, so independent of space, time and money, that it could occur only under the pressure of the most stringent necessity and with access to sources of most remarkable mental and physical energies.

Such was C I A M in the years of its greatest influence and so was its last-coming member, the M A R S group of England. Arising nearly spontaneously, as I have said earlier, to identify and defend a nexus of ideas on architecture in the contemporary English situation, and joining with the larger movement as it rose to its own occasion, it overcame the varied and unequal temperaments and talents of its members under the necessity it shared with C I A M to understand the new programme and the new responses to it that it saw before it.

Apart from the performances in deeds and words of its members it achieved in its short life two important objectives, the first a clear exposition of its ideas in the form of an Exhibition that took place in the Burlington Galleries in 1937; and the second a plan for London which opened up a stream of new ideas and underlined the necessity for a comprehensive view of the eternal problem of the great city.

I cannot think of C I A M apart from le Corbusier. He dominated it by being more of it than any other member, by giving it both its long-term objectives and a methodology with which to reach them, by raising it to its moments of poetry, and sustaining its organisation by his courage in adversity and his belief in the certainties of art. I can remember my feelings upon first meeting him at La Sarras being exactly as described by Maurice Jardot;*

My Work, le Corbusier (translated by James Palmes), Architectural Press, 1961.

He does not have the open expression and the easy smile of
those who readily inspire sympathy; animation and grace are
lacking; the eyes are dull, the voice is flat and uneven. But
candour and strength reinforce an impressive demeanour
seemingly built for defence, behind which he appears to
withdraw, to watch and to observe. It is very hard not to feel
respect and curiosity.

I have spoken earlier of the apparatus of a dedicated architect and
in doing so thought often of this man burdened with his immense
talent of which at times he appeared to be more the guardian than
the possessor, so warily did he move in the world of affairs, so
detached from any conflicts of personalities that so often stirred the
surface of CIAM, but coming to his decisions and pronouncements
with such uncompromising force, with such access of disdain for
base considerations as shocked even those who thought to understand them.

Thus he saw himself sometimes as Don Quixote and sometimes
as *l'animal de fiacre*, the work slave of his ideas, and this with a wry
smile that used to take my heart because it stood for the sort of
modesty which kept him clear of whatever might do damage to the
gift he served.

He came to architecture through art. But no. He never forsook
art. He embraced architecture, with art, designing his first building
at the age of seventeen and then soaked himself with the art and
architecture of Europe, Greece and Asia Minor; drawing, measuring, observing and remembering.

Thus when he came to the decisive years of his contributions to
L'Esprit Nouveau (first number 1920) he had served a hard
apprenticeship to Auguste Perret, the practical innovator of reinforced concrete, had met Ozenfant the painter, who opened new
prospects to the young architect, and made, through painting, the
deepest incursions into the revelation of light and form which were
to sustain him in his life to follow.

23 The Fagus Factory, by
Walter Gropius, 1911. The
prototype of all industrial
architecture to come.

24 The Bauhaus, Dessau, Germany, 1925, by Walter Gropius. The workshop wing. A rigorous exercise in industrial method.

25 The first metal stacking chairs, by Marcel Breuer. One of the earliest decisive models produced by the Bauhaus.

26 The Turgendhat Haus, Brno, by Mies van der Rohe. The classicist of the movement exhibiting his propensity for dwelling on the type solution.

27 Interior of the Turgendhat Haus. A model for the ruling élite – perfected in the materials of its time, and disposed in patterns fixed by the mental rigours of its creator.

right
30 The Swiss Pavilion, Cité Universitaire, by le Corbusier, 1930-31. A prototype for all purposes.

31 The Sanatorium at Paimio, Finland, by Alvar Aalto, 1932. An imaginative thrust into the industrialised future, directed by function and the structure of reinforced concrete.

28 Villa Stein at Garches, France, by le Corbusier, 1927. An example of 'the modern aesthetic at its sparkling best.' Sculptural architecture disciplined by function.

29 The villa Savoye, Poissy, France, by le Corbusier, 1929. The fully developed style in action. A functional monument set in a rough meadow.

32 Laminated plywood chairs in series, by Alvar Aalto.

33 Accoustic ceiling in the library, Viipuri, Finland, by Alvar Aalto, exhibiting an imaginative affinity between waves of sound and the properties of plywood.

34 Photograph of a model of the Cité d'Affaires building, Algiers, by le Corbusier, in which can be seen the struggle between plastic form and machine regimentation.

35 Housing in Siemenstadt, Berlin, 1929, by Walter Gropius. Housing used on the scale of a city rather than a suburb.

36 Perspective drawing of le Plan Voisin, Paris, by le Corbusier, 1929. The first appearance of the massive skyscraper solution to urban density.

37 Photograph of a model of the plan of Nemours, by le Corbusier, expressing the beauty of integrated function released by virtue of its office.

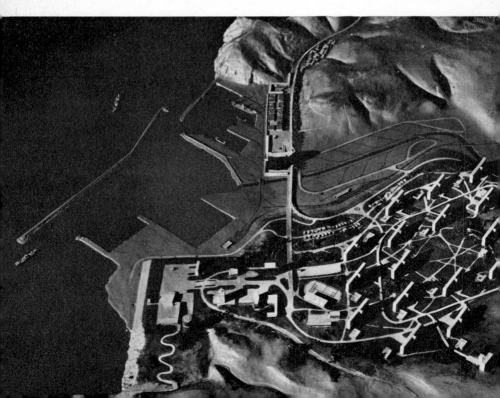

I will refer again to the apparatus of a dedicated architect, in le Corbusier that of a genius, but to distinguish it from the pigmy efforts of state sponsored semi-science purporting to investigate this and that aspect of the contemporary situation. It is one of the supreme mysteries of the human brain that it can at the same time sustain a mass of unequal data with sequences of connected ideas drawn from them, to be reigned over by massive deductions, logically satisfying, and yet united in germinal forms recognisable as art. So rare and spectacular in its effects is this type of mind that it is commonly written off as unaccountable genius when in fact it is but the full flowering of a type of mind which both in its greatest and in its more normal forms is immensely useful to society, and never more so than at this moment when too great a reliance upon technocracy and low forms of logic have depressed its value in mens' eyes.

Le Corbusier possessed a gift for passionate observations which must earlier on in his life have been directed by the peculiar bent of his mind, as indeed is always the case in persons of genius, and serves to explain his talent for what might be called the grand analysis. The early stages of the creative process rest upon this gift of observation and arrangement, so alike in all arts. In him it widened to a view of what was occurring in the wide world of modern urbanism and what had brought it to birth. That particular story Sigfried Giedion told in two massive books from which the lessons pointed by le Corbusier are irrefutably proven.* But they had not been written when le Corbusier spoke of 'the eyes which see not' and invited the world to survey its own creations with a new eye.

Two great deductions can be made from it. The first that if we would save our cities we must use what technology has given us to separate and use each for the virtue in it, the powers of locomotion and the capacity for high concentrated building, so that, secondly, but all of a piece with it, we may secure again freedom for both car

* *Space, Time and Architecture*, Harvard University Press, 4th edition 1962; and *Mechanization takes Command*, New York University Press, 1948.

and pedestrian and our ancient and immemorial rights to sun, air and verdure.

In 1921 Pierre Jeanneret, le Corbusier's cousin, joined him, and behind the great projects of urbanism and the pronouncements that issued from the pages of *L'Esprit Nouveau* (and came together in 1923 in the world-accepted book *Vers une Architecture* – Towards a New Architecture) there lay the foundations of a life of ceaseless toil, the self-appointed burden of the nobleman of ideas who is the only true aristocrat of the modern world.

Vers une Architecture describes the circumstances and set the tasks for a new epoch in the environment of western man, and characteristically it starts by reminding architects of the fundamental and eternal truths of mass, surface, plan and order. I have carried with me over the years an impression derived from his exhortation to laymen that they should use their eyes and trust their senses in recognizing that the forms of industry – grain silos, bridges, aeroplanes, motor cars – are the engineer's manifestations of a new art, the product of close selection, based on the logic governing the statement of the problem and its realisation. 'The problem of the house,' he wrote, 'has not been stated. Nevertheless there exist standards for the dwelling. Machinery contains in itself the factor of economy which makes for selection. *The house is a machine for living in.*'

This nearly fatal last statement, that echoes in wildly varying modulation through the period, needs the qualification which opens his argument for the fusion of the two approaches to building.

The Engineer inspired by the law of Economy and governed by mathematical calculations puts us in accord with universal law. He achieves Harmony.

The Architect, by his arrangement of forms realises an order which is a pure creation of the spirit . . . he affects our senses . . . and provokes plastic emotions; by the relationships which he creates he wakes profound echoes in us, he

gives us the measure of an order . . . in accordance with that
of our world, he determines the movement of our heart and of
our understanding; it is then we experience the sense of
beauty.*

The greater part of the book is taken up by his admonitions to
architects to remember clearly that the elements of architecture of
mass surface, plan and order – 'Architecture is the masterly, correct
and magnificent play of masses brought together in light' (How it
reminds me of Vanbrugh!) – are the great simplicities underlying all
architectural form, whether of Egypt, Greece or Rome, and that
they may be worked once again through the geometrical construc-
tions of the engineers and with the logic of a new statement of needs.

These chapters, read again after many years, are like a very
particular sort of history of mediterranean architecture in which
each example illuminates the beautiful principles discovered by a
young man in fulfilment of the as yet but vaguely apprehended tasks
placed upon him, many of them not to be achieved until he had
broken through the arduous mental struggle with the mechanics of
living that lay between him and his personal but inevitable achievement. They are followed by a series of suggestions that, though
presented in a dry and unemotional line, nearly obscured the rich
architectural message of the earlier pages by the force of their
impact, none more so than the proposition to replace a central
quarter of Paris by a group of mathematically aligned skyscrapers
of really vast dimensions complete with their infrastructure of
elevated motorways, below which are glimpsed the parks and
pedestrian ways of the liberated earth.

This was a proposal which left entirely out of account the social
and political stages which could serve to bring it about, and it
repelled by its near brutality. Nor in the schemes which followed in
later years for Algiers and Nemours, so much more sculptural and
organic and so closely related to the necessities of site and landscape

* *Towards a New Architecture*, le Corbusier (translated by F. Etchells), Architectural
Press, 1927.

and to the demands of a possible economy, was there any real social basis capable of bringing them to birth without at the same time sacrificing the very liberties their author would hold dear.

Yet in the sense of telling the world what to do about its cities they were practical. We will reclaim the lost art of building cities only when we discover the true nature of the forces underlying their generation, and learn how to manipulate them in terms of art. Le Corbusier did not turn away from these forces; if anything he exaggerated them: and he had to imagine for himself a society capable of both creating and using them.

It was in that sense that superior architects accepted them, and it was for this that he was called to South America to bring to birth, through the direct infection of his prophetic imagination, what the world has since acknowledged to be a Renaissance of the arts of building and planning. His meeting with Lucio Costa and Oscar Niemeyer, from which the celebrated Ministry of Education building, with its so definite tropical character, was the direct outcome, encouraged a school of architects, artists and landscape architects to create a fusion of native art and skills with the rationale of modern European-based architecture which gave form and coherence to the aspirations of a nation still in process of formation. It appeared to the world that Brazil had suddenly assumed a character not hitherto associated with it, pointing to the truth of the assertion that the true uses of architecture are to give form and significance to what life should be; to point, in this case, to a possible destiny.

To set against the list of plans and buildings unrealised, including the League of Nations building at Geneva – won in competition and disqualified by professional spite – he completed two houses and a hostel which magnetised the creative field of architecture everywhere.

The Stein house at Garches was built in 1927. It is, as he himself describes it, an example of 'the modern aesthetic at its sparkling best', for without in any way distorting the structural validities of reinforced concrete, and accepting the disciplines of an emerging industrial technique, it has a sculptural form the most satisfying in terms of depth and movement suggesting the possibilities of an elegant life. Yet in the strictest formal, even mathematical, relationship, it is a serene yet deeply stirring work of a man at the height of his powers (plate 28).

The Villa Savoye at Poissy, built in 1929 is a work more heavily loaded than the last, its living floor raised on *pilotis* and carrying above it an arrangement of walls screening terrace spaces to provide spacious sculptural forms of essentially monumental character (plate 29). The domestic arrangements, connected by both stairs and a double ramp, are patrician, but they recall the life of the studio, as do so many of his houses. As we first saw it in photograph, the geometric statement in the midst of the rough meadow, it was an enigma not fully resolved, tantalising and mysterious, and appearing to serve a life with which we had few connections. It appears to me now to be of the essence of mediterranean culture with its roots in an archaic part.

To realise the laughably eclectic nationalism of the Cité Universitaire, founded upon Patrick Geddes' belief in a noble internationalism, is to describe the most unlikely setting for the most remarkable of these three buildings, the Swiss Pavilion, built 1930-31 (plate 30). It consists of several floors of students' rooms rationally disposed behind light curtain walls and carried entirely free of the ground on a line of twinned *pilotis*, with a staircase and service core rising clear from a podium of social accommodation so as to expose the functional anatomy of an essentially simple building in the clearest way possible, a sculptural work answerable at every point for the validity of its presence.

Its surface textural range advances to include at one extreme a precisely articulated screen wall of window and rigid panel and at the other a curved wall of random stone, so that the muscular display of bare structural form heightened by primary contrasts of light and shade is further enriched by contrasts of texture.

The inauguration ceremony was like a funeral, but it was the birth of a prototype to be reproduced ten thousand times from

Highgate to Tokyo, the anatomy of the international style, the child of the Hiltons replacing classical Hotel Georges Cinqs in every capital of the world. Here in Beirut where I write at this moment I see the unlikely offspring of this imaginative thrust into the future in endless and mindless reproduction over the lovely indentations of this antique coastline, an item in the steady obliteration of identity that encircles the Mediterranean like a fatal rash of shingles.

These three buildings are the fruits of the most controlled and fertile period of le Corbusier's creative genius. Independent though he was at all times, these buildings were done while he still belonged to a creative group actively searching in the social and economic framework of their societies for the true limits, the imposed restraints from which the form of an urbanistic architecture could draw an inevitable and enduring corroboration.

Either it was not in le Corbusier's mission to find it in France, or France failed to provide it as she failed him in so many appeals to her rigid intellectual *amour propre*. But this was not so elsewhere. We have seen how far Germany had come in the twenties to meet Walter Gropius' approach to industry in the Bauhaus, and in the highly organised and socially-minded states of Holland and Scandinavia the ground was even further prepared for the reception of ideas that affected the environment of urban living over a wide range and in particular detail.

The work of Dudok in Holland and of Ragnar Östberg in Sweden had made an emotional appeal to England in the twenties, leaving its mark on the London Underground stations of Charles Holden and the Town Hall of Norwich, to name but two examples, to be reinforced later by Asplunds' haunting and half-classical Library at Stockholm which he was happy to refer back to Sir John Soane's Bank of England.

There was something in the rational organisation of society in correspondence with the relatively undisturbed growth of a well-founded body of taste in these regions that had made the acceptance of what was revolutionary in France appear natural and proper. It was not so much a question of a new start as what to do next; and there is the presumption that works as seemingly apart as Stockholm Town Hall and the Van Nelle factory in Rotterdam were both citizen-inspired and the product of closely integrated societies aware of the direction in which they were moving. One felt this strongly in Östberg's Town Hall, but the patron of the Van Nelle factory, my *beau idéal* of European intellect in action, was vitally concerned in his evolving environment, as was later to be proved in the rebuilding of Rotterdam.

It was in the late thirties on my way to Finland that I came upon a clue, due difference given to its harmonious collaboration with nature, that was entirely constructed of contemporary elements to the most beautiful reinforcement of my faith in the new order we proposed.

> Again in Stockholm on the way to the airport there was a moment when the contemporary rhythm was most strongly established. A wide road had passed over a railway and was sinking to ground level. On the left were sports fields surrounding a wide-spanned building housing tennis courts, and the setting for the whole was diversified of rocks, trees and occasional houses. It is hard to say in what way this pattern of natural and artificial structure evoked so marked a feeling of harmonious exhilaration, but something in the tempo of the swiftly moving highway set a long beat which was echoed in the smooth span of the sports building and carried on again in one after another smaller detail: of balustrade, lamp standard and the like; while the lines of the road and of the building were as completely congruous as though, to use McColl's simile, they had been cut in one pattern on ice by a single skater. I can remember vividly the impression it gave of belonging to me and my generation and how the truth of this filled me in the momentary glimpse that came as I passed over it in the plane a few minutes later.*

* *Fine Building*, Maxwell Fry, Faber, 1944.

The well-being of Scandinavia unsettles the British who are unused to so comprehensive an organisation of the environment of living. 'What does Swedish perfectionism lead to beside the highest suicide rate in Europe?' they say, oblivious of their background of uncoordinated visual squalor. And they say it with suppressed trepidation, and cease to say it when they arrive in Finland, because though it ought to apply there it does not seem to. This small country of lakes and forests of pine thinning off towards the Arctic Sea exists now, as then, under the shadow of the USSR, but maintains, perhaps because of this, a fresh and vigorous form of democracy. They are, they will tell you, 'wood' Finns who are the real inhabitants of the region, and Swedish Finns who keep the books.

I do not know to which class the older Saarinen who built the railway station in Helsinki belonged, but Alvar Aalto, in whose works the Modern Movement became dramatically explicit in the early thirties, is a 'wood' Finn, a man firmly based and emotionally rich.

When I came to Finland in 1938 to work on the new town of Petsamo that, because of its rich nickel mine, was taken over by the Russians after the bitterly contested war with Finland, I found in the sanatorium at Paimio (plate 31) and in the comprehensively-planned mills and town of Sunila forms that staggered me by the force of their imaginative thrust into the industrialised future. It might have been the fierce contrast of sun and snow with dark foliage and steely lake water in which these singing buildings were set, yet I cannot have been mistaken in the vigour to which the clarity of their structure so beautifully contributed.

I came across some early works of Aalto's in Obo, square buildings decorated with classical ornaments faintly inscribed as though they were the last imprints from an old mould. These buildings were still, as it were, encased, and by contrast the sanatorium, not so many miles away, was like a bird released.

Lyricism is a rare gift among architects. It is a capacity for song such as is to be found in the early works of Marcel Breuer. It signifies some lightness of touch; but it may also appear, as in Aalto's work throughout his life, as an absence of solemnity, or more positively as an entirely healthy element of celebration.

Aalto operated at all levels, as an architect should. He designed not only the great factory at Sunila, but the township of its employees; and out of the plywood that issued from the mills he designed furniture, using principles of manufacture that it patently embodied: and this furniture, like that of Mies van der Rohe in stainless steel, became the prototype that replaced nearly all others (plate 32).

For the lecture room of his library at Vipuri, now destroyed, he designed a timber ceiling foreshadowing his later development, but remarkable in providing for acoustical sufficiency by a form so beautifully suggestive of the waves of sound, so flattering to the properties of a wood skin, and so joyful in itself, as to mark it off from all other artistic manifestations of the movement as being the work of a mind moving in a direction all its own, towards solutions lying outside the movement's fairly restricted range (plate 33).

The Movement contained, of course, a wide assortment of temperament within its ranks, but the main lines of its advance followed certain groupings of interest, among the first of which was that of Gropius and Mies van der Rohe being the most closely bound to the announced collaboration with industry.

Though le Corbusier in his book *Vers une Architecture* has a deal to say about the need for collaboration and the debt architects owe to industrial form, Gropius and Mies meant it and acted accordingly; Gropius by founding the Bauhaus, and Mies by using nearly exclusively the products of industry. And both men understood the properties of steel and glass and were sympathetic towards their limitations. Both were patient long-term workers; the one a collaborator, and the other a lone dog; and each in his way effected a revolution.

Though le Corbusier was in the end the most influential member of the group, in the early days he lacked the national background that gave an air of solidity to each advance registered in Germany or Sweden.

It took France his lifetime to recognise his genius and as le Corbusier obviously set store upon recognition in the city and country of his adoption the isolation he felt spoke through the stentorian, disdainful tones of his books and pamphlets from the pages of which we were able to follow the earlier progress of his remarkable talent.

Then he was a man of many parts – painter, sculptor, poet, publicist, prophet and architect rolled in one. 'To understand my architecture,' he said, 'you must look at my art.' This was by no means as easy or as open to explanation as he made out, for his earliest works such as his houses at the Weissenhof Siedlung were barely distinguishable from the others, and there was but a gradual metamorphosis from his standard 'domino' houses to the still highly disciplined though more freely modelled houses of Garches and Savoie.

The Swiss Pavilion of 1930-32, though it broke free from *l'angle droit*, was a highly disciplined work, however extravagantly conceived; and it was successful. It was, perhaps, the tantalising design for *le cité d'affaires* at Algiers that announced the nature of a struggle existing between his plastic sense and the necessary stringencies of the industrial programme (plate 34). The tall shaft of this otherwise typical office building is composed, not of a series of equal window openings expressed by the frame as in the Ministry of Education Building in Rio he was to do with Oscar Niemeyer in 1937, but is heavily patterned or modelled in openings that were a form of *brise-soleil* bracketing over several stories, and giving to the model, which is all we have of this building, the rich, chased effect of a Mediaeval reliquary.

It is indeed a lovely work that might well have found its testing occasion in the UN Building he never built; and for that building he also made a model in which such a treatment is foreseen, a model that makes one weep for what might have been, though I have to remember that, faced with the same problem in the horizontal secretariat in Chandigarh, his attempts at modelling broke the ship's back, as you might say.

Though reinforced concrete was le Corbusier's chosen material, and his early use of it was in advance of his engineer master Auguste Perret, he used it as any artist would, for effect; unlike the artist-engineer Maillart or the as yet unrecognised Luigi Nervi in whose works the modelling of structure was the outcome of a semi-logically directed system of selection.

I have no quarrel with either. Purity or impurity of intention or achievement are relative terms when considering the accumulation of experience that gathers into a movement that will change the world's attitude towards architecture.

Scandinavia was always apart it seemed to me, looking back on the meetings of CIAM; not, be it said, for any deficiency of promise or performance, for these countries had social and governmental structures more favourable for the development of a new architecture than most; but on account perhaps of their very self-sufficiency that enabled them to perfect techniques of a high standard in which craft was valued, and to continue therefore, without loss of energy, traditions of workmanship nearly abandoned elsewhere.

While, of course, everything to me was influenced by the already acknowledged masters in Europe, the variety of expression had to include the heavy-handed Mendelsohn, the lyricists Asplund, Breuer and van der Flught, the romanticist Scharoun, and the towering classicist Mies van der Rohe himself, for in no other way could the movement explore the outer limits of its territory or prepare for whatever departures from its common achievement the future held in store for it.

However tempted I am to recall the buildings of individual architects of the pre-war period, and realising how little I have spoken of the English contribution, my main task in this chapter is to give you some lively appreciation of the true nature and the scope of the architects' revolution so that you may assess its value to us in our present situation.

To bring out the rich flavour of what was done I have used the acknowledged leaders as representative of the movement, and in so doing have kept close to history, what though at lower levels work as typical and as good was being done.

But I must now refer to the urban structure into which the individual buildings fitted and against which unfailingly they were seen. The notion that no building was sufficient unto itself permeated the thought and guided the discussions of CIAM which normally took place against the background of a large *grille* that not only accommodated the practical programmes of participating groups, but defined the mental disciplines that confined them.

This *grille* was a device of le Corbusier's that provided us with a graphic analysis of the subject matter of our discussions while at the same time locating the studies and projects put forward by member groups. It occupied a large wall, and as the map of a theatre of war is to a war cabinet, so was this *grille* for us. The chief components of urban activity – work, living, recreation, and communication were drawn from the biologically directed analysis of that remarkable Scotsman Patrick Geddes to whom we are all indebted for theories and principles based on the idea of growth and organism as opposed to the static or the romantic notions hitherto entertained.

It must be remembered that, until Ebenezer Howard put forward his rather simple diagram of a garden city, no one for a century had thought about the nature of cities, of what they were composed, how they grew, what gave them character, and what differentiated one from another.

Since John Wood laid out Bath, James Craig the New Town of Edinburgh, or John Nash completed the truly remarkable fabric of his developments for Regency London, the idea that towns should be planned, that their growth might be guided and contained, or that they could by any stretch of the fancy be regarded as works of art, had ceased to be entertained.

The nineteenth century market commodity of land, like most else in that period, was regulated, if at all, only for the curtailment of abuses so flagrant as to endanger health on a large scale. And this obtained well into this century.

That it should now be otherwise we are indebted primarily to Ruskin and William Morris, for up to their time reform was directed to prevent abuse, to raise standards of public hygiene, and make buildings safer; but without offering any workable alternative to *laissez faire*. These two were reformers of a different kind. They were artists and visionaries, and it matters little now that, turning from a system they disliked and distrusted, they should plunge into the middle ages in search of their Grail.

The first Hampstead Garden Suburb that was the delayed child of their imagination was much less Gothic than the Houses of Parliament, for though the units of which it was composed looked mediaeval enough, their internal planning made an end of the Victorian parlour and introduced to the world 'the lounge', the informal twentieth-century living room that fitted our new psyches like a glove. And they were built of good pleasant honest materials, and taken together, in detail and in the main, this suburb was intended to be and was accepted as a single work of art.

As a model for twentieth-century use it suffered by turning from the urban idea to one of a *rus in urbe*. Ruskin disliked the Renaissance equally with industrialism. His golden age lay somewhere in the twelfth century.

As a result English town planning that expanded out of the garden suburb has maintained to this day an anti-urban bias, and it became the responsibility of CIAM to show that within the context of twentieth-century industrialism, using its structures and materials but not its methods, reliable urban structures of high artistic integrity were not only possible, but necessary.

It is not to be imagined that this could be the task of architects alone, for the composition of the Bauhaus, or the connection between say, the architect Rietveld and the painter Mondrian, would discover upon how wide an artistic front the movement advanced.

Then also the work of the artist-engineers, from Freyssinet to

Nervi, exposing the new capacities of metals and reinforced concrete, the bridge builders, the skyscraper builders perfecting the instruments that made possible the release of the vast creative energy of the period: all these, added to the emergent knowledge concerning therapy, the workings of the mind and the subconscious, converged upon the attempts to create a new structure for urban living.

From 1923 onward to the Nazi domination of Germany a group of architects that included Ernst May, Gropius, Mies van der Rohe, Wagner and Bruno and Max Taut, built housing schemes, mainly for the under-privileged, that by the rationality of their conception, the breadth of their treatment and the fineness of their detail proved them the models of an urban form in which an industrialised society could find disciplines in harmony with their circumstances in Europe (plate 35).

They were, unlike the traditional apartment development of Germany, of modest height, indeed the sort of terraces that we could handle in England today, but used on the scale of a city rather than a suburb, and capable of being rationalised for production in series.

It is a mistake to think that a city needs a great variety of unit models. The West End of London was made out of minor variations on a single plan, small for the poor, large for the rich, and repeated in terraces of lengths that shock our weak nerves today, yet salted with terminal variations, and arranged in visually satisfying layouts that unify the whole.

Quite recently I came upon largish areas of Tel Aviv, which must have been built in the thirties, of three-storey apartment units that could have figured in the Weissenhof Siedlung of 1927 and were repeated endlessly by speculative builders, each adding his small variation of treatment, along spacious tree-lined streets and boulevards, and proving to me this anxiety for difference to be irrelevant and destructive of background civic harmony. One of the truest signs of decadence is weak nerves.

Gropius edged his schemes towards an even more rational expression of straight-line industrialism, investigating in the process the relation between height and sunlight penetration that lies at the core of the subject, yet without loss of urbanity.

I cannot over-estimate the value of this great practical exposition that took place in Weimar Germany and of which the lessons are yet fully to be learnt, because I must set it beside the more daring and in some ways more complete projects of le Corbusier, that were to remain largely hypothetical.

He attacked the city with weapons drawn from its own armoury, and the attack, unmodified and humanised by the process of execution, remains in the pages of his early books as challenging, didactic, and uncompromising as it came to us so long ago.

I have spoken earlier of how from his analysis of urban congestion in America he selected the means of release from it in terms of the concentrated skyscraper, the separation of pedestrian from vehicular traffic, and the balance of concentration by a ground surface returned to its happiest use as verdure played over by sunlight. This is the revolution exposed in his spidery line, the terms of the complete problem that traffic engineering refused to face up to in America or elsewhere.

In his Plan Voisin for the right bank of the Seine at Paris, done in 1925 (plate 36) he returned to the charge; and again in 1937 varied his attack with improved models of the same weapons, and in vain, never getting further in the proof of his theories than the single block of the Unité d'Habitation at Marseilles (plate 39), but what a proof!

These projects also suffered by being only a part of a city, where in his great plan for Algiers, in that of Nemours, and in the compact little project for Saint-Dié, done after the war and outside the context of this chapter, his ideas were expressed with finality.

But Nemours exposes with utter clarity the beauty of true function released for the virtue of its office – the separation of the elements of contemporary life operating to their greatest advantage, to them as for us, in a plan that draws our admiration as a thing of beauty in itself, but only because it makes explicit in terms of art the living organism of a human machine for living (plate 37).

How much useless and ignorant malice has been unleashed by journalists incapable of recognising the fundamental bases for an enjoyable life in the twentieth century in deriding the use of these key words to a better future. Have I to say again, thirty years after we opened our architect eyes to the modern world: can you not see? Can you not see?

6 The post-war years

The effects of the Second World War were terrible in ways made possible by science: the outcome, signalled by the bomb of Hiroshima, leaves us with a legacy of terror. What took place could be thought to have deprived us of our faith in science as a vehicle of human understanding, or of the capacity of human understanding itself.

We have, nevertheless, in accordance with whatever governs our actions, continued to live under the constant threat of extinction, and contrived once again to think as hopefully as possible about the unending problem of how to live together in peace and amity and in the fulfilment of our dreams.

In the last chapter I spoke of the *rapprochement* between modern architects and industry in the sanguine terms proper to that period when the first results of Bauhaus teaching, the early pronouncements of le Corbusier, and the examples of a new architecture in Europe appeared to light the Western world with the hope of creating life afresh. And I emphasised the importance, with the deeply persuasive nature of its finest works, of the rational system of analysis upon which these works were built, the value of a rational programme imaginatively interpreted.

It had seemed to us at that time that this rational basis for archi-

tecture and urbanism, derived from science itself, and a bridge therefore between architecture and industry, was the basis for an architecture *capable de tout*. No longer restricted by matters of taste; no
longer tied to an historical past, it was free to find its own aesthetic
out of programmes arising directly from the irrefutable circumstances
of the time and from the materials and structures of the industrial
system. Finally this architectural revolution seemed to have been
drawn from and to flourish best in that liberal-technical climate that
was the essence of Europe.

The post-war period discussed in this talk is going to reduce these
claims by placing new obstacles to their fulfilment; by assailing their
logic; and in one or another way making them obsolete, or appearing
to, which may be another matter.

Firstly, the industry to which Walter Gropius made his first
approaches has grown not in size only but in its relation to the community; in the extent to which it penetrates everyday life and doing
so tends towards depersonalisation through the curtailment of spontaneity and variety.

Then science, from being the highest employment of our best
inquiring minds – from being, that is, the best that is in us – dispersed
its powers in specialisation and allied itself with the powers of destruction so as to give the impression to ordinary people of following
with but unequal zeal the opportunities offered by the study of biology
and humanity itself.

Thus, it is not that the gesture made by the architects in the
inter-war period has been rejected, but rather that it has been absorbed with the indifferent ease with which a busy executive accepts
the suggestion of an underling, leaving less trace than its importance
warrants.

The enormous death-roll of the war had little effect upon world
population which in response to preventive medicine, better food,
and renewed hope, continued to rise and to offer to reproductive
machinery expanding markets to justify its explosive philosophy.
Coincident with this numerical expansion, the rise of the masses to

the acquisition of the full range of material benefits – at least in Europe and America, and to the practice of government through one or another forms of violence, have put a new and sinister gloss on the notion of democracy.

Within the building industry, of which the architect is the natural leader, the pressure of technocracy has patently affected the basically humanistic direction of the architect and obscured his vision with the multiplication of semi-scientific apparatus and the false ethic of material efficiency.

It has been a triumph for numbers and mechanical production against reason and a human proportion, and science, cut off by its absorption with physics and specialisation, has taken a negative attitude to an affair that seems to concern it so little. But architecture and urbanism have now become positive and dominant elements of twentieth-century culture. Is it possible that science, which flourished in liberalism, can neglect them without loss of ultimate purpose? Can it pursue a life without taste? Is science also succumbing to the Caliban it fathered?

I must return to the architectural story which is first a record of dispersal from Germany and Central Europe to the ends of the earth, but first to England and America. Of the three principal figures Gropius, after a brief sojourn in England as my partner, went on to Harvard and a group practice in Cambridge. Mies van der Rohe became a Professor of Architecture at Chicago and rose again in strength to set standards for an ideal technocratic architecture; while le Corbusier, lay low during the occupation, but like many another in this posture went on thinking.

The change of scene gave Mies van der Rohe the opportunity to build the skyscrapers he had dreamed of. It took time, but since there was never a sign of hurry in his nature, this can only have been for the good. For the University of Illinois at Chicago he built a campus the total effect of which is somewhat arid except for the architecture building which is so beautiful as to want, said a local wit, a religion of its own to go in it. Its beauty arises, as in the Turgendhat

Haus, from an exalted sense of function and an innermost awareness of the virtues of modern materials. Like the Turgendhat Haus it is haunted by classical nostalgia, more temple than building, and its effect on American architecture has been profound.

Designing the two Lakeshore Drive apartments, from the austerity of which he drew the last ounce of compressed emotion; and the Seagram Building, New York (plate 38), where he sought to cast a glow (a 'brazen' glow, would it be?) over a final exposition of refined technocracy, he set the highest possible standards for the realisation of a monumental 'fix' for American civilisation. 'I will give you,' he is reported to have said, 'the soul of technocracy'. It is something to be remembered.

For Walter Gropius the situation was not so merciful. American civilisation gave Mies van der Rohe his chance, but for Gropius, I have the impression, America was too vast, busy and multifarious, and Harvard too gentlemanly. He gathered his students, he formed his co-operative, he made many buildings, he spoke, he wrote, but nothing was the same again. The Bauhaus, re-established by his disciple Moholy-Nagy at Chicago, attracted the amount of attention accorded to a new rite in decadent Rome and faded quietly away. His contacts with Konrad Wachsmann over a system of industrialised housing centred on the vexed question of variable dimensions, proved idealistic, and failed. There remained his indomitable courage, his inflexible ideals, and his glorious record as an example to youth, but this can never have satisfied him.

For le Corbusier the story was a continuation of frustration and triumph, of a rich creative life continuing to dwell on the great themes of urbanism and architecture, but drawing constantly away from the earliest contact with day-to-day reality in accentuation of the inconsistencies of his character, towards his obsessions with painting and sculpture, towards the less disciplined, more personal aspects of architecture considered only as an art.

During the occupation he founded ASCORAL (*Assemblée de Constructeurs pour une Rénovation Architecturale*) as an instrument for the implementation of his ideas on urbanism and industry, and with the return of peace made abortive plans for Nemours and Saint-Dié, saw his hopes for a new Algiers eclipsed; but found solid ground, but only too little of it, on which to complete the Unité at Marseilles (plate 39), the first large building in which to enclose the germinal ideas of his Ville Radieuse.

After incredibly frustrating labours it was achieved, and became immediately a place of pilgrimage, but whether it proved its point – whether in spite of its sun and air it is a suitable vehicle for the raising of families and healthy social intercourse, is still unsolved. There are ten of them built and the doubt still hovers. But there is no doubt as to the beauty of the building or of the intense feelings it evokes.

A further, and a quite catastrophic, set-back awaited him in New York, where after assuming the undoubted leadership of a team of experts that was to site and then build a headquarters for the United Nations, his design was not so much set aside as swallowed up into a New York architectural processing plant to which the site of the building was attached.

What the world might have seen, what le Corbusier might have done to set beside the grandeur of Mies van der Rohe, we will never know. His *maquette* tells us something. His skyscraper of Algiers tells us more. We sense that it would have been an ultimate challenge at the technocratic centre of the world for a man bent upon wringing from industrialism a sense of spontaneity and variety, things foreign to its real nature, and the imprint of man rather than the machine. It would have been his apotheosis. It might have changed the current of American life. But the machine civilisation swallowed him as it swallowed Gropius, and he retired baffled and deeply wounded.

At Bogotá in the forties he was again engaged in grand urbanism, this time with his disciple José Luis Sert; and in 1950, when we were instrumental in bringing him into the Chandigarh project in a position of power and authority, he was working on the design of the votive chapel at Ronchamps, and had a small model to show us. His idea at that time was to build it of an inner and outer skin of expanded metal on a light metal framework and cover this with 'gunnite', i.e. concrete forced on under pressure.

It makes no difference to the approach to the design that it was finally made of concrete, for it still consists of an interior and an exterior with no logical structural connection between the two. It gives the impression of great solidity, of immensely thick walls pierced by tiny windows splayed on the inside in mediaeval fashion. In fact the walls are as hollow as they would be on a film set and the roof is I know not what. Undoubtedly a *tour de force* of sculptural expression on the outside and a brilliant essay of nostalgic regurgitation within, it yet darkens my architectural horizon and I am glad that there is only one of its kind.

By comparison the plan of Chandigarh is firmly rooted in society and its logic follows along lines of growth (see plate 9 in chapter 2). Remembering that it was designed for an impoverished state in the North of India without the resources for separated traffic ways or high buildings, and without even the traffic to use them as yet, it proposed a solution that caters for a greater range of human activity than any other plan I know of, and remains a work of art.

The classification of roads into the famous seven Vs, the partition of the sectors into the two opposing activities of life, the disposition of entry, major circulating, and ceremonial roads, of city and cultural centres, and the placing of the state buildings, display the coincidence of logic and feeling that gives the city its air of grand inevitability. Its major lines were settled, as I have recorded earlier, in a few days, but it is the work of a lifetime.

The grandeur of the Capitol group of buildings has eclipsed the greater merits of the plan. They must be taken together as a monumental group and compared only with the similarly grandiose display of Brasilia. They exhibit the growing divergence in le Corbusier of programme and structure from architectural concept, which is to say, in respect of the High Court and the Assembly building, that the programme has been interpreted on the level of grandeur, of a concept projecting forward into time as a monumental work of art rather than something at the scale of present circumstances.

Within this framework these buildings are superb monuments, especially the High Court, though nobody is going to make me admire an untreated face of inert concrete. What my eyes tell me I will respect. Nor can I agree that the irruption of official consequence in the form of balconies and recesses in the length of the Secretariat building is architecturally successful. The one is not compatible with the other. Either you take out the superior function and deal with it separately, or sink it in the repetitive mass.

My admiration for le Corbusier's work goes a very long way. His contribution exceeds that of any other architect nearly at any time in history. I am still under the necessity of finding a direction for architecture generally, and from this point of view I am not alone in regretting an excess of art over function, or, as in the case of the Textile Owners Building at Ahmedabad an exaggeration of function. The over-grandeur once admitted, as on view it quickly is, the houses and the museum in the same city became achievements of a high order, to be taken to the heart and cherished.

I have not seen the monastery at La Tourette. It would seem to have offered him a programme of stark and inflexible grandeur suited to the monk he was, and to have brought out the best in him; and I have yet to see his building in the midst of Harvard.

His influence has been worldwide, first as an analyst and prognosticator, and as the originator of a nearly mosaic law enshrined in CIAM, but finally as the resurgence of the Mediterranean mind dwelling in beauty and reproducing itself in one after another lovable building, the inspiration of succeeding generations.

Before following in the track of le Corbusier's influence to countries as far apart in every way as Brazil and Japan I must make a final comment on that curious work, *The Modulor*, upon which he set such store, for unlike those who brush it and the mathematical series upon which it is based away, as having nothing to do with architecture, I see the connections between art and mathematics as being of unceasing interest in a time when the complexity that surrounds them will be gainsaid in favour of apparently simpler but in fact more sterile explanations. To acknowledge the connection and to seek the means of incorporating it within the creative methodology of architecture was a task the importance of which comparative failure hardly lessens, since we must come to it again in the future as we continue to meditate upon the proportioning of what we externalise in building: it belongs to the very heart of our matter.

It was in 1937 that le Corbusier was called to South America, and he describes the journey in passages that evoke the magic of air travel at heights at which we were still in some contact with the earth below. His visit, and the Ministry of Education Building in Rio that he made with his disciple Oscar Niemeyer, transformed the architecture of that continent by releasing the creative energies of a group of young architects, and a genius of a landscape gardener Burle Marx, for a range of building – houses, office buildings, churches, educational buildings and housing on a scale reminiscent of but more grandiose than that of Weimar Germany: an architecture capable of anything, but strongly marked by the character of its country of origin. Under a government that later fell from power the capital of the city was moved five hundred miles into the interior and laid out on a new site to the plan of Lucio Costa and with the architecture of Oscar Niemeyer.

This plan, won in open competition and of which I only escaped being a judge by being too occupied elsewhere, could be regarded as being the realisation of le Corbusier's Ville Radieuse, composed as it was of massive apartment buildings, high and low, set in ample open ground and connected by highly developed motorways with a vast point of interchange on the axis of the aerodynamic layout. This strongly-marked axis shot off towards a capitol group of buildings bordering a great lake in which Niemeyer forsook the sinuous plasticity of the architecture he and his companions had developed to match the climatic and cultural conditions of the country, in favour of an elementally geometric monumentality of great size and consequence, but deprived of much of the human reference to be found in le Corbusier's comparable group at Chandigarh and pointing perhaps to some difference of temperament, not only between the two architects but between their government clients.

That Japan, with its ancient tradition of meticulously proportioned domesticity and the archaic simplicity of its garden shrines, should find itself launched upon a course of *brute* concrete buildings rivalling the master's in thrust and scale, can best be explained by the need for a forceful expression of the realisation of new-found vigour arising from the re-established identity of a nation defeated in the upward movement of its destiny. This is what these buildings of Kenzo Tange, Makawa and an active school of architects beside stand for: they are celebrations that with exaggerations appropriate to the emotional climate in which they are conceived, house the social and governmental activities of a country in ferment of activity, and leading, therefore, to the rapid but consolidating evolution of a Japanese architecture that traces its origins to the earlier ferment of the thirties in Europe.

Faced with the growing urban concentration of population explosion as violent as anywhere in the world, served with an advanced technocratic equipment, and given this joyful outburst of intense creative activity, it is to Japan that we may look for the solution of the problems of urbanism that are vital to our continued occupation of the world; the major problems of our time.

Removed from the Mediterranean arena dominated by le Corbusier the Scandinavian countries, led by architects of the distinguished calibre of Asplund and Markelius of Sweden, Jacobsen of Denmark, and the quite exceptional genius of Aalto of Finland, pursued a course supported by a public recognition of architecture found nowhere else in the world, and by the fusion of an immaculate craftsmanship with the most advanced building technique; making in the whole a social intelligence of quivering sensibility.

The contribution that Scandinavia has made to the cultural level of European domesticity, on the evidence of England at least, is something for which we are entirely grateful. But like all good exports it is the expression of internal well-being and harks back to that sumptuously simple city hall of Stockholm to which Ragnar Östberg called the liveliest talents of his time, and stimulated thereby the patronage of Frank Pick, the father of the London Underground and the first client of English modern architecture.

Quite early in the thirties Stockholm solved a tangled knot of traffic interchange with the most elegant piece of road macaroni to be found, a multi-level dance of traffic weaving its way out of the centre. And this was the predecessor of the Vällingby multi-level solution to the centre of a suburban relief city based on rapid transit and completed with an elegant harmony of disposed building form, and the Hötorget concentrated urban complex in the centre of Stockholm, freed for pedestrians.

Little of this could have been achieved if the citizens had not conferred upon the Government the power to own land extensively and to become, in their name, the prime developer and co-ordinator of the urban environment. Lacking such sense and reality of owner- ship, with all the responsibilities it entails, planning knocks itself against the wall of dissipated self-interest and fails.

Finland offers evidence of a similar accord between the parties of contemporary social and cultural development; with the same re- markable fusion of interests, of skills and achievements at the many levels of a strangely united population, to which – as perhaps in no other country would it be so possible – Alvar Aalto ministers as a cultural *alter ego*.

Now this is a beautiful thing to see, for it argues a degree of general understanding of a general situation to which we should all wish to aspire. There is no hope of real quality without the existence of a strong body of taste in the active section of society, and an understanding of what activates an environment, upon what kind of day-to-day decisions it depends, is best promoted through example as also by the comparative lack of what could blur the outlines or lower the importance of what art and artefacts have to impart.

Alvar Aalto's earlier work, as clear and lyrical as anything the movement created, contained elements of future importance to his art, but for his country also. Without regressing on his talent, but out of a rich life that followed its natural bent engrossing what was germane to it – the materials and skills native and beloved by his country, the strong sense of a recognisable community – he fused his functional architecture with a saving grace that gave it continuity in time, and allowing him the closest contact with the true nature of his problems, in physical as in human terms. The free forms he evolved are so much in line with that acoustic ceiling in the Viipuri Library; the texture of them is so much in harmony, so much of a piece with what Finland stands for. His work has an originality as unstrived for as that of Cézanne discovering the true nature of the Mont Ste Victoire country. It is much more to my fancy than the Sydney Opera House, and has more to tell us concerning our own situation in England.

It may be allowed to say a few words about our own experience in the tropics of south-west Africa, to which I was consigned on an overcrowded troopship in 1942, and where I devoted with Jane Drew and our companions in the enterprise some fifteen years of effort to extract an architecture from the trying climatic conditions of that lovely region.

We came upon a colonial life relatively untouched by time or war: we left sovereign states involved with the politics and technocracies of the outer world, and were thus the witnesses and the agents of very great changes, some of which we could only regret. We found few building materials we could use, no building industry, no codes of building practice worth the name, and little architecture we could emulate. But everywhere in the huts, villages and mud-walled towns of these trusting, gentle people we found the beauties of a once closely-adjusted culture that was melting away before our eyes.

The analysis we made of our problem was dominated by the climatic necessity for moving air passing under shade across buildings held like open fingers to receive it. The abundant timber was rapidly destroyed by termites, and great ranges of diurnal temperature split open any sizeable areas of reinforced concrete roof which, alternatively, released its captive day-time heat in the already sultry night hours.

What emerged from long trial and error was a perforated architecture of cast concrete screens held into the prevailing trade winds, coloured in the non-bleaching shade, and diversified in texture by the use of a low-grade granite rock, shot with vivid streaks of colour, that we quarried wherever we could find it.

Our favourite contractors were Italians working as family units in a contact with Africans as close as we ourselves liked to be, and, like us, outside the pale of officialdom; for whatever may have been the rational conclusions to which we came concerning the nature of our architecture, its character could only be the measure of our absorption into the African scene.

Such as it was it underlined the truth, still too little regarded in the architecture of Europe, that climate is a determinant in the order of building as it is in so much else in the dry and humid climates; and this we have tried to establish in what books we have written on the subject* and by founding the only serious school of tropical architecture and planning in the world as a department of the Architectural Association in London, presided over by Dr Otto Königsberger, our friend in so much of what we tried to do.

Since our first tentative essays in the forties West Africa has entered the industrial world of power politics with overcrowded cities to which the combined efforts of architects and planners of many persuasions bring only a marginal amelioration. The conflict between the wish to emulate the technological patterns of the west, and the need for a slower but firmer base for cultural and political advance, is to be found all over the developing world, and throws into relief the dichotomy present in our own.

In the USA the high pressure technocratic scene was dominated

*Tropical Architecture, Jane Drew & Maxwell Fry, Batsford, 1964. *Village Planning in the Tropics*, Jane Drew, Lund Humphries, 1947.

by Mies van der Rohe, with his more workaday counterpart in the firm of Skidmore Owen and Merrill, rising also to high levels in such buildings as the Lever Building, and to excellence in the Manufacturers Trust Building on Fifth Avenue. It was a level at which Eero Saarinen took an honourable place with his still over-ambitious General Motors Research lay-out, the pursuit of a technocratic ideal of immaculate high efficiency, an image of modern America.

That level was not held for long. Whether as an image it was insufficient, or whether the over-abundance of the economy had to find its counterpart in architecture, the leading architects of the country, led by Saarinen, began to indulge themselves with an increasingly extravagant series of solutions for the standard problems of university and public buildings generally.

I do not think that le Corbusier's example had anything to do with this North American phenomenon, or very little, but one of its stimuli stemmed from a sort of engineer's play with form, as evidence for instance in the warped surfaces of Eduardo Catalano, but as offered in general by the extension of free engineer structure reaching out to its possibilities as a coverer of space. These possibilities were being exploited in Italy by two engineer-constructors of great stature, Pier Luigi Nervi and Luigi Mirando. Nervi, the greater innovator and more sensitive artist of the two, had evolved systems of construction so close to nature, so absolutely responsive to the surge and flow of contained forces as to assume a life in his buildings nearer to the idea of an organic architecture than anything of Frank Lloyd Wright's. His buildings were for simple needs – hangars, exhibition buildings, stadia – but this only served to isolate their qualities.

The fragile vaulted forms of Félix Candela, small and inconsequential besides Nervi's great structures, seemed to have been drawn directly from growing form; while the warped surfaces of Eduardo Catalano, made up of straights, were touched with the sort of logical abstraction with which Buckminster Fuller has fascinated his followers, but which are not to my mind the real material of architecture.

In all, these excursions of the engineers amount to a substantial extension of the possibilities of modern structure, away from the straight line boundaries of space of the early period of modern architecture towards a plasticity governed by a richer and more complicated discipline. And the architects' first reactions to this breakaway, coinciding with a need of their own for a breakaway of some sort, have been startling and indiscreet. Saarinen's Kresge Hall at MIT is a curious scaleless object with an interior fitted into it with no more success than that of Stubbings Congress Hall in Berlin, and in the sports building at Yale the failure to assimilate the engineering form is still more marked.

These engineer forms are not easy to assimilate because they are original works that justify themselves in their own terms. They call for serious collaboration rather than plagiarism, and serious consideration on the part of the architect, because some of the forms, those of Catalano in particular, are extremely violent without being reassuring.

But what we are now seeing in the United States is something other than imitation. The fantasies of architects such as Paul Rudolph and Yamasaki, or Saarinen in his Idlewild terminal building, are not prompted by engineers but are the fantasies of a rich world, exuberances made for willing spenders, by men for whom CIAM and the Bauhaus are the half-forgotten legends of old Europe, and these buildings gleam like orchids in the spiritless monotony of an endlessly industrialised urbanism.

The European breakaway from the smooth white image of the early CIAM period is fairly directly ascribable to the vaulted brick and concrete house, the Maison Jaoul of le Corbusier that touched off a side stream of nostalgic yearning for the type of 'Instinctive Architecture' described in the opening talk, the simple, rough-grained, honest, anti-machine image that Rayner Banham played with for a time as the 'new brutalism', an expression set in motion by le Corbusier's use of the term *béton brut*. In the hands of certain Dutch architects it earned its title, and could justifiably describe a good deal of the fierce heavily industrial structures of steel, brick and untreated concrete so well handled by architects such as Erno Goldfinger and the Smithsons. But domesticated in England it quickly became romanticised into a sort of Lowry Lancashire image as in James Stirling's housing at Preston, and finished up as Brighton University and Churchill College, rough honest brickwork, arches in solid concrete and lavish white painted soft wood, at a time when such things should have been driven out of existence by mechanisation and high wages!

As the machine invades further channels of everyday existence, ironing out the marks of individual eccentricity everywhere, the architects and artists react against it. Sir Kenneth Clark, in a paper entitled 'The Blot and the Diagram' sees the artists exploring their subconscious in a series of 'blot and dribble paintings' represented by, it should be noted, the New York painter Jackson Pollock; and the architects, on abundant evidence from any city in the world, tracing their future in rectilinear Mondrian diagrams.

But it is not so. The revolt is shared by all artists. Nor is it entirely negative, however disappointed with the results Sir Kenneth may be. It is a genuine exploration prompted by the extension of science: through Einstein into the unmeasurable; through Freud and Jung into the subconscious. It is an extremely frustrating exploration through what Henry Adams called the 'super-sensuous sea of chaos' to which as long ago as 1910 he saw science as being reduced, and in nothing is it more frustrating than its lack of form and definition. Artists point to this and that sense of unity in their works, but with all the will in the world we are often hard put to find it. Despite the best intentions it remains at the exploratory stage, bereft of programme, form or definition.

There are attempts in progress to take architecture the same way. The Guggenheim Museum of Frank Lloyd Wright is an expression of feeling to which structure has been made to conform, the works of Pancho Guedes of Lourenço Marques, harking back to Gaudi, are more emotional than substantial. The Sydney Opera House of

Utzon is nearly hysterically lyrical to the breaking point of its supporting structure, and the laboratories at Philadelphia and the Unitarian Church of Louis Kahn are forms of personal emotion supported by the most far-fetched of theories that nevertheless find an answering echo in every anxious young student adrift in the cross current of architectural opinion.

The reasonable logic of the Bauhaus is at a discount. It seems as though architecture is in search of symbols rather than solutions, and that the symbol uppermost in our mind is an irrational one though it tears the architectural programme to fragments.

But this also is not quite true. We have seen three master architects starting out on the same road and finishing up far away from each other, yet each successfully pursuing an aspect of architecture; at any one time there must exist a variety of temperaments and attitudes which it would be impossible to confine within a so-called international style.

Oscar Niemeyer defends the extravagances of Brazilian architecture by pointing to the non-industrial background of Brazil, the unbalanced state of society set against the opportunities for architects of courageous *élan*, which opens another level of variations on what nevertheless remains a central architectural theme. 'Our desire', he said in describing the project for the highly symbolised modern Art Museum at Caracas, Venezuela, 'was to develop a compact form detaching itself clearly from the landscape and expressing in the purity of its lines the forms of architecture whatever might be happening to the rest of the arts'; which is nearly exactly what le Corbusier's Maison Savoye, standing there in its meadow of a garden, set out to do, and did. Lucia Costa, who could be described as Niemeyer's better half, is no less definite and concise. The form of Brasilia is as definite as a machine, the curves of the plan playing with the cones and boxes of its third dimension in a manner as contemporary as the car it serves, but symbolised as its head with geometric forms as old as time.

By comparison Chandigarh belongs to an elderly world, which in

44 The Library, Ibadan
University, Western Nigeria,
by Fry Drew & Partners.
Architecture of the 'breathing
wall', involving a direct
collaboration with climate.

45 T.W.A. Terminal Building,
Idlewild Airport, New York,
U.S.A., by Eero Saarinen.
Architect-engineer architecture,
exploiting the possibilities of
reinforced concrete for function
and effect.

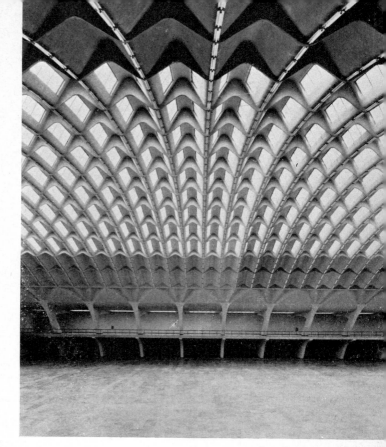

46 Exhibition Hall,
Turin, by the
engineer–architect,
Luigi Nervi,
showing an affinity
between structural
concrete and
natural form.

47 The Unitarian
Church, Boston,
by Louis Kahn.
An example of a
new architecture of
symbol and emotion,
seeking deeper
levels of functional
justification.

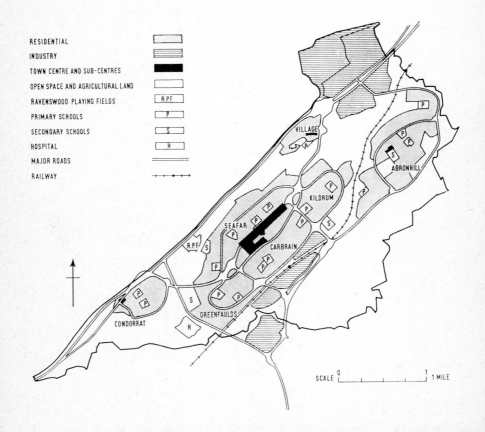

RESIDENTIAL

INDUSTRY

TOWN CENTRE AND SUB-CENTRES

OPEN SPACE AND AGRICULTURAL LAND

RAVENSWOOD PLAYING FIELDS   R.P.F.

PRIMARY SCHOOLS   P

SECONDARY SCHOOLS   S

HOSPITAL   H

MAJOR ROADS

RAILWAY

VILLAGE

ABRONHILL

KILDRUM

SEAFAR

CARBRAIN

CONDORRAT

GREENFAULDS

SCALE 0 _____ 1 MILE

48 Photograph of model of Cumbernauld New Town, by Hugh Wilson & Associates. The comprehensive idea in a new town considered as a single work of art.

49 Plan of Cumbernauld New Town, showing the interdependence of pedestrian and wheeled traffic and the central exchange machine at the cente.

50 George Stephenson College of Further Education, Watford, by the Hertfordshire County Architects Department. An industrialised building in an industralised setting.

51 Housing at Harlow New Town by Michael Neylan. A partly nostalgic return to the emotional responses of 'rough hewn' materials originally prompted by le Corbusier's experiments with mixed materials.

52 The machine triumphs in
commercial captivity. An office
scene in Westminster, London.

fact it does; an older, poorer, less hopeful and an altogether un-mechanical world. Chandigarh kicks against the machine, as a comparison between the secretariat buildings of each capital will quickly prove.

One may now discern in the rapidly-evolving pattern two main direction thrusts, neither of them exhausted. The first accepts the industrial situation: this is the line of Gropius, Mies van der Rohe, the Brazilians, Arne Jacobson and the Scandinavians. The second reacts against it; this is the line of le Corbusier, the 'new brutalists' and the American fancy boys, unfairly bracketed together.

Outside them, but deriving more from the former than the latter, the great constructing world moves on with the blind force of a natural act, using what comes to its hand, thinking and acting from day to day, destroying and building up regardless of form. This is the story of the great cities everywhere, of the urbanising country-side, the tourist-ridden coast lines, the beauty spots engulfed and obliterated.

It is our chief concern, and to round off the story of architectural development up to the present time we must follow the course of town planning at levels less dramatic than Chandigarh and Brasilia but more pertinent to our main theme.

The interest centres on Great Britain in its attempt to ease the pressure on central London and to confine its increasing spread by establishing a ring of new and self-sufficing towns in a girdle some thirty miles from the centre. It was the aim of the exercise to draw off industries from congested sites in East London, and to attract industries that would otherwise have settled in London, providing both with a population of young workers living in ideal surroundings, the sort of life that an advanced technological civilisation could pro-vide, separated by areas of inviolable countryside from the bad old city.

It was Ebenezer Howard's garden city in an advanced and com-plete form, with all the benefits accruing from long experience, the accumulated detailed knowledge with respect to road layouts, open space, provision for schools, shops and centralised facilities.

Each town was run on a liberal but businesslike footing by an autonomous corporation with public representation and an adequate technical staff, and these towns are what their organisations made of them, successful within their limitations, financially successful, and hitting their targets with increasing accuracy as time went on; a series of full-size practical experiments in the art of living.

Initially there were six New Towns round London and one ill-fated town, Peterlee, on the Durham coal fields. But further towns have since been added, notably Cumbernauld to cope with Glasgow overspill, and Hook, at a distance of about sixty miles from London, jettisoned for political reasons at a late stage in its conception. There are more to come.

The first thing to notice about these New Towns is that they are comprehensive entities taking place on complete sites, surrounded by protected agricultural land. They might gather round an existing village but this does not invalidate the comprehensive nature of their conception, the interdependence of all parts and functions of them, or the necessity to think comprehensively of people living and working together under twentieth-century conditions.

The early New Towns fail by being insufficiently urban. Haunted by the long-established image of the garden city based on the opportunity presented by modern transport to flee from the town and live ideally in the country, they have been established at densities too low to create urban cohesion. They occupy too much land and too feebly even to look like towns when you move about in them. The image is unvigorous and sentimental even at the centre. The Crawley town centre reminds me of a Walt Disney toy town; it is not architecturally serious enough. But the experience is there. These towns have been workshops of experimental research into comprehensive town building, and at Cumbernauld the attempt has been made to create a technological town based on real human needs, the pedestrian as a reality rather than a figment, the community using its transport rather than being used by it (plates 48 and 49).

Hook went on to deal with the relationship of industry to the town, correcting early mistakes made elsewhere, and to solve, as at Cumbernauld, the complicated problem of drawing people and transport into a town centre without dislocation, of handling concentration without friction, without unnerving pressure, of harmonising the conflicting interests that gather round dense aggregations of people.

What took place in Britain took note of the experience of the Swedes at Vällingby, of the Dutch in their new towns on the reclaimed Zuyder Zee, and of Europe in general, since Europe long before it becomes a political entity will have learned to share its vitality. And the workshop of the New Towns was really centred in London, where the London County Council, with its immense load of creative work, had perfected an organisation for dealing as comprehensively as possible with a problem only to be realised by fitting together a kaleidoscope of fragmented opportunities into the conspectus of a single ideal. In its developments on the fringes of Richmond Park, and notably at Roehampton, the LCC put its accumulated experience into the comprehensive development of a large area of beautiful land with high and low building, point blocks and slab blocks. The architecture is fashionably rough and uncouth, with too much exposed concrete for my liking, but the total effect looks like town building for the twentieth century.

So too is the new housing at Sheffield, with the added advantage that it makes its impact on a sizeable but not immeasurably large city, heavily modelled in ridges with valleys running down into it from surrounding moorland. Industry cluttered up the valleys in the nineteenth century, but its larger units are moving out on to free sites beyond the city. New housing therefore crowns the heights and leaves the valleys to be cleared for streamlined parks leading up from the city on to the moors. My first terrible impression of Sheffield, gained many years ago, is being eradicated. It appears now to be a town that may become as beautiful as it was once ugly, efficient for all purposes.

The village colleges of Cambridgeshire, the school programme of Hertfordshire CLASP (the local authority self-help building consortium inaugurated at Nottingham), all point in the same direction without as yet having formed a public opinion strong enough to deal with the general situation.

The political flavour of Britain is favourable to the great enterprise. It is not only the curious mixture of public control and private enterprise of the welfare state that helps us, but the liberal philosophy that remains with us, the morality that makes us feel responsible for society, not only in the mass, but in loving and individual detail. This is something that, cherished by the exercise of such works, appears to me to justify our best hopes for a successful emergence from the dilemma in which we find ourselves.

The Americans coined the phrase 'urban renewal' to describe a surgical operation on the congested heart of a great city. The congestion was effected long ago by rail and subway transport. Motor car traffic aggravated it, and highway engineering, acting unilaterally, made a nightmare of it.

The centre of Brasilia is a traffic interchange which can be regarded as disappointing, but the centres of American urban renewal are by force of the stagnated situation, pedestrian. Worshipping their cars as they do, the Americans have been invited out of them to shop in Victor Gruen's suburban pedestrian centres which have come into existence because the urban centres are unapproachable: and *ordered* out of them in these centres themselves. Their surprise at finding themselves in family groups afoot in the shopping labyrinth is one of the pleasures of a visit there.

I do not intend to dwell on the merits of any one of the schemes for great American cities. They are, both in America and here, but partial solutions of the problems of urban rejuvenation at large, cutting a dash and making a profit at the centre, but leaving the total problem unsolved. We may feel grateful that we see the possibility of renewal. If the powers generated through science and industry are to serve us for something better than destruction it is for us now to draw up the programme for a new man-made world in its entirety.

But the fragmentation of attitude on the part of architects, which I referred to as the symptom of an American affluent society, has its counterpart here in a revolt from what was seen by the breakaway group that preceded the dissolution of CIAM to be the over-simplification of the synthesis of industrialised architecture in the early works of the movement. In fact it is deeper than this objection and runs perhaps parallel with le Corbusier's mounting distaste for American technocracy, for the combined onslaught of technocracy and beaurocracy that he feared above all else.

The pure logic of this situation is to be found everywhere expressed in the monotony of the commercially exploited window wall of the typical office building in which anti-social finance expended itself until it was halted. Nobody really cared for this solution, which the public referred to as 'match-box' architecture, realising little of the dumb pressure of the anonymous forces that brought it about.

On all hands there was a hankering for the touch and sight of structures and materials un-reminiscent of the machine, for 'things counter, original, spare, strange', for the qualities that I found in the 'Instinctive Architecture' of my opening chapter.

And thus at the moment, when one side of the profession was locking itself securely into the machine, the other was escaping from it. At the moment when mechanised architecture was seen as the only vehicle for the vast programme of housing and urban renewal, the means of evading the outcome were being sought, either by giving to the industrialised prefabrication of the parts of building the brute and massive strength of an antique post and beam architecture; or by re-newing the search for a solution using the extraordinary versatility of structural brickwork to achieve the same end, being led by this process to overcome the pressures of high density by tortured labyrinths of romanticised alleys and courtyards from which the rationale of sun-light and space was virtually banished. It never rains but it pours!

Not that I believe this to be more than a temporary aberration, sanguine and healthy in origin, pointing to an aspect of the matter that we can by no means disregard, but modified by the great size and weight of the problem expressed in the programmes for new and renewed urbanism to match our growing population: a problem reproduced the world over.

It is bedevilled by two major considerations: the containment of motor traffic, and the humanisation of machine architecture. What is to be the form and structure of it? Tightly constrained as in Arthur Ling's ingenious Runcorn plan? regionally realised as in the Southampton study? lineally disposed as in the south-eastern proposals? or aerially interlocked in structural or vegetative complexes such as the Japanese propose?

These are but examples of the creative possibilities latent in what Rayner Banham calls 'the second machine age', if for one moment they can be given their rightful place above the self-destroying anxieties of the modern scene.

Plans such as these can be taken as imaginative descriptions of future possible lives under conditions in process of evolution but not yet fulfilled; and if they suffer from a lack of certainty as to the nature of the instruments they employ in terms of novel forms of transport, degrees of mechanisation, of obsolescence, etc., they reflect what troubles us all, but what inevitably, we must resolve.

The main problems of mechanised building have either been solved or are clear to us, on the experience of Scandinavia and France, from where the best systems derive. But this is only to say that we know how to transfer the main load of building from the scaffold to the factory, on the site or away from it: the technical problem has been solved, but at the expense of much texture; contrast and rhythm, by means of which architecture communicates with us.

The advantages even in the architect-controlled systems originating in the Hertfordshire Schools Programme, and given a new twist and a wider range by the Nottingham Consortium, betray their machine nature, not only in a certain inflexibility at the joints, but by reason of their interruption of the creative process by being more a kit of parts than material for architecture.

The approach of the Yorkshire Development Group, centred about the rationalisation of a set of plan forms on an eighteen foot frontage, places the horse – cart-horse though it must be – more clearly in the shafts, and is a more acceptable regulator in large quantities of urban building.*

In all this we are being driven, like so much else of which contemporary life is composed, by the pressure of the repetitive machine seeking to overcome the high costs of living it engenders, towards a final rationalisation that would leave architects free only to select the limited number of parts in what could inevitably be a pre-determined environment; as the housewife moving in a false-roseate light down the package-filled aisles of the supermarket towards the cash desk, finds her choice, wide though it may seem, circumscribed by the imagination of the great corporations of which she is, in military terms, the target.

That is our situation in England as we move towards the realisation of an urban programme that strains our resources of money and manpower, and what troubles many of us, on the evidence of what has so far been done, is the element of inhumanity in it, the difficulty we see in leading it into the harmony of a total environment.

*Even here practice fails to confirm theory since the architecture is mediocre and the Group will not cohere.

7 The present

This history of the development of architecture from the early years of the century to the present is going to offer us, when we see it clearly, the means of dealing with matters of broader concern than architecture itself.

But I must first take you back to reconsider the state of architecture in those early years of the century. Despite the excellence of individual architects it was class-ridden, academic and backward-looking, with one outlet only to society in the garden city movement initiated by William Morris and propagated by Raymond Unwin. It operated in a restricted field as a form of narrow professionalism. And this was true of both the Continent and America, for it was one of the defects of culture in the nineteenth century that it flourished in one only of Disraeli's two societies. Granted with Bernard Shaw that it is a disgrace to be poor and that you cannot make an interesting play about uninteresting people, you equally cannot make two societies look like one, and when finally you come to consider how society is to live in the twentieth century it is with a single society that you must deal.

You may look at it in another way in recording the emergence of what was the unrepresented working class to a much fuller affirmation of citizenship, a levelling of class society; or in still another way as the revolt of the masses. Whatever way you look at it, the broad problem of how to live successfully in the twentieth century concerns the whole of society considered as one; and if there is a religion – apart from the wavering belief in the omnipotence of physics – that is held today by an important section of society, it is the feeling that we are responsible for our fellow creatures.

When therefore Walter Gropius turned his back on the arts and crafts movement and made the first direct overtures to industry through the Bauhaus he was performing a unifying operation for much more than architecture. 'The Bauhaus was inaugurated in 1919,' he has written 'with the specific object of realising a modern architectonic art, which like human nature was meant to be all-embracing in its scope', and of CIAM he said, 'that this small supra-national group of architects felt the necessity . . . to see the many-sided problems that confronted them as a totality'.

From this time forward architecture ceased to be the instrument of a privileged class. It ceased even to be architecture in the sense in which it had been for so long regarded, for at one end of the Bauhaus curriculum it was industrial design and at the other end urbanism, laying itself open to be whatever was concerned with social environment by whatever means lay open to be used. And the models that the Bauhaus made for industry, the simple furniture and the light fittings that have remained the prototypes of domestic design, like the great patterns of housing that Gropius contributed after he had left the Bauhaus, had all of them, as Herbert Read pointed out in his timely work *Art and Industry*,* the likeness of a technocratic exactitude in tune with the spirit of the time.

Gropius had found in fact the means of harmonising the products of the system, however large, however small, with art. He had done what Ruskin and Morris, what all artist-reformers had wished to do, not so much by trying to raise the level of industry to that of art, as by, in a way, humbling himself to recognise in industry the

*Art and Industry, Sir Herbert Read, Faber, 1966 (revised edn.).

materials, methods and skills out of which an art could emerge without deformation or self-consciousness.

What he saw was an art arising from the virtues of the system, a machine art in so far as it was the product of the machine, but one of which the full value could be extracted only by those not limited by the narrowness of specialisation, by, in fact, artists of comprehension.

This explains why he brought with him into the Bauhaus artists such as Paul Klee and Kandinsky. The industrial system has by definition excluded artists. The combination of industrialism and successful materialism had, as we have seen, elevated the fine arts to a ridiculous pinnacle out of the reach of ordinary people. Shut off into museums and carrying price labels of astronomical value, the works of the past, even the works of the so recent past as Impressionism, became a sort of privileged currency, while art schools served only to turn out art teachers for lack of a true patronage with something to celebrate.

But the creative impulse is not confined to art, nor does art come when it is called for, as the art schools bear witness. Art can emerge, as we have seen in our study of 'Instinctive Architecture', from very humble and humdrum circumstances provided that the circumstances are fully understood and incorporated into the creative effort.

The creative impulse is a manifestation of the urge for survival, of nature's admonition to continue, and it takes a very wide variety of forms arising from the need to adapt our circumstances to our successful survival. The creative impulse is in fact so normal a human activity as to become diverted when specified as art, for it is in essence both the fulfilment of an instinct to survive and its recognition. This same impulse now prompts the awakening dwellers in English slums to prettify their house fronts with highly coloured paints; the manifestation announcing quite clearly that they mean to take an interest in their lives which up to now have been reckoned as of no more account than items in an economy.

The immense preponderance of science and its application as industry must, as human activities, have attracted or just swept into them a great deal of creative talent. They are in themselves of course a creative act, the great creative act of the age that has multiplied not only the possibilities open to man, but also the number of mankind able to enjoy those possibilities.

One may discern both in science and industry the creative and artistic talent at work reconstituting and unifying their advance. Such figures when they emerge are men of a comprehensive talent, in the proper sense of the word cultured, and if Einstein may serve as an example it could be said, to quote Ortega y Gasset:

> that he needed to saturate himself with Kant and Mach before he could reach his own keen synthesis. Kant and Mach – the names are mere symbols of the enormous mass of philosophic and psychological thought which has influenced Einstein – have served to liberate his mind and leave the way open for his innovation.*

But the point I wish seriously to make is that having entered science or industry the person of anything less than abnormal creative or artistic talent is absorbed into a specialised arm of either system, gets to know a very great deal about that specialisation, and as a result tends to be an ignoramus about everything else, and an opinionated ignoramus into the bargain. To quote y Gasset again,

> The most immediate result of this unbalanced specialisation has been that today, when there are more 'scientists' than ever, there are much fewer 'cultured' men than, for example, about 1750. And the worst of it is that with these turnspits of science not even the real progress of science itself is assured.

The crisis in science could rest upon just such a premise, but it is more than that and overflows into the system, now so vast as to be indistinguishable from life itself, that it has built round it, a system

* *The revolt of the masses*, Ortega y Gasset, Allen and Unwin, 1951.

that must be made accountable for the millions of new population for which there is no predictable future, and for the unquenchable outpouring of mere matter bereft of feeling, emotion, or any good human use whatsoever. This is the real hell of a situation that we all in one or another way acknowledge.

I have dealt with aspects of this critical situation that lies to be solved by architecture and urbanism, but must still reconsider what place there is in the world of thought and action for an approach that depends upon specialisation only in the arrangement of the facts upon which creation and judgement depends. I will go on to define a person of taste, which relatively few people even aspire to be today, or a person of 'culture' which too many people imagine themselves on the strength of their entirely fragmentary knowledge to be, as essentially one capable of harmonising the conflicting facts of existence in the light of comprehensive thought.

By this definition only artists are cultured, and this is very nearly true, and perhaps always was. But in so far as we are in great need of people of taste and culture, even more are we in need of standards to which persons of taste and culture might properly aspire, I would say that the capacity to think comprehensively, searching for the full cycle in the solitary event, to refer events to their effects upon society, returning always to the human reference, rank high in the list of requisite virtues.

A man of taste in the eighteenth century knew the classics and could talk about Renaissance painting. A man of culture in the twentieth century, if he has the nerve to pretend to such a claim against the torrent of second-rate art-nonsense poured forth by every vehicle of mass taste and entertainment, if he has the pretension to live and act his culture with even a little of the responsibility that fell to his eighteenth century counterpart, must be aware of architecture and urbanism as the dominant arts of his time, must meet me on the level at which I discuss the contributions of the great figures of our art, and understand the liberating force that has flowed from the conjugation in architecture of art and science.

The New Town of Edinburgh, like the City of Bath, was created in the image of Greece and Rome recalling in its forms, however politely domesticated, the circuses, rotundas, and coliseums of the classical times to which it aspired. To what may we aspire today?

The one great end of our time is to find a form in which we may successfully survive. The alternative to this can be none other than disintegration. A philosophy that puts its faith in nothing more than the further and further exploration of physical matter, from the earth to the moon, from the moon to the galaxies, explorations un-related, without centre, concerned with matter and power, leads us further away from the real heart of the matter that lies within us, and is still as large as the universe.

It is not my intention to propose either a new religion or a philosophy. I have laid before you in as much detail as I can muster the workings of a major human activity which must be regarded as an art to which science contributes thought.

I remember many years ago Sir Owen Williams proposing a motion for debate. 'When I think,' he said, 'I am an engineer (scientist?). When I cease to think I am the master of the works, I am an architect.' Now it is true that architecture, in being an art, is concerned with doing rather than thinking, but you cannot arrive at the form of a building or a city or a society, come to that, by thinking only, or calculation only. You can think about this and that aspect of it; you can make calculations and assumptions, have theories and hypotheses, work out lowest common denominators and coefficients of many useful kinds; but still you can arrive at only partial solutions of partial aspects of it; still it is something unconnected with the central problem, which is to arrive at a form that being deeply impregnated by all the circumstances that may each be the subject matter of thought and calculation, can finally be arrived at only through a process of feeling and imagination, failing which it is useless for human needs.

It is useless because this process which I described to you earlier

as being in the last resort incapable of analysis is essentially transcendental. It is more than the sum of its parts. It is religious because
though it concerns man and uses matter, its final outcome depends
upon neither, but is a revelation.

The intense effort by means of which a work of art achieves unity,
the harmonising of all the elements of which it is composed, is a
measure of its usefulness, for it is through the pleasure that the
recognition of this unity evokes in us that we are able to accept the
new form in which life shall continue, and adjust ourselves accordingly.

The shock of recognition is beyond ignorant people whose habits
are disturbed, and the chief social value of persons of taste and
culture lies in their receiving the true impression made by new works
of art, and reassuring their fellow beings.

Let us say again therefore that our chief aim is to find the form
in which our life may successfully continue, and in doing so search
not so much for an ever-expanding physical universe as for what
may confine and define the form of human life, since there is no
form without limitation and definition.

This at least is the aim of the great art we now contemplate, and
is its compass very much less than life itself? So much less that it
cannot serve for model, for some measurement of what should
discipline the world of technics, or even of science itself?

I described in chapter four the emotional climate in which
modern architecture was born and struggled to find itself up to this
time present. It was a talk that I found difficult, even distasteful, to
compose because I could find in it so little that I could genuinely
celebrate. What the scientists had to tell me of their researches into
the composition of the physical universe had little of comfort for
humanity; yet society, having in the first flush of these successful
discoveries taken to its bosom the immense hope of an outcome
through the natural sciences, having for all working purposes made
a philosophy out of this mistaken idea of progress, was in process of
disintegration when compared with its former state, a fragmentation

of personality now recognised as afflicting the body of science and society alike.

What stood out for me in this study, what one after another author insisted upon, was the increasing formlessness of society, as registered in the formlessness of typical urban sprawl everywhere in the technocratic world. It was as though the phenomenal increase in the speed of every form of communication was negatived by an increase of uninformed numbers of people and by a mass of un-identifiable matter that prevented cohesion. It was as though the struggle to establish forms of order which we call civilisation, cultures relevant to the circumstances, were being constantly defeated by the process of entropy, the tendency of things to revert to mere mass, or matter, or grass, to something without value.

Deep at the base of this great technocratic idea that was supposed to bring such comfort to humanity I had to suspect an error, and that error, in so far as I can isolate it, springs from a lack of whole-ness, a lack of heart, it must be said. There is no heart in the matter.

Let me now go on in a very practical way to bring up to date the picture of our occupation of the steadily shrinking globe starting with our own island.

Without troubling you with statistics, which exist in greater quantity than our knowledge of what to do with them, I will point to the growth of London in a hundred and fifty years from a popula-tion of under a million to its present incalculable size, incalculable because it is no longer a city but a region, a central activity with vast peripheral effects which we are unable to deal with if we continue to think of London as a city.

Cobbett called it the 'great Wen', which is a more or less permanent tumour, because he couldn't comfortably walk from one end to another of it. Now it is too large to think of.

Our attempts to limit it by confining new growth to satellite New Towns have failed. It continues itself to grow in size and in intensity, and its growth is now registered in sleepy towns and villages as far away as King's Lynn and Thetford, and colours and future of south-east England as a population pressure on every part of it, made up of a natural but formidable increase, an immigration from elsewhere (meaning the north) and an unspecified exploitation due to its situation between London and the Common Market (win or lose). The reality of this situation frightened the Committee set up to examine it as it must frighten anyone who can recognise the effects of mere numbers on an established occupation of land.

It is not a question of what we can put up with, inured as we are to ugliness and incoherence, for there comes a point when if we are unable to cope with the problem we lose all. It is the point where population increase becomes of no value and life loses its point because it has lost its form.

We come now to think in terms of the region rather than the city, but we have not mentally reached that point yet. Le Corbusier developed through ASCORAL a theory of lineal deployment of industry linked in a triple thread of rail, road and water and following the lines of European valley beds. This lineal work-city came to nodal points of exchange and market in towns of concentrated texture commanding both the interconnecting lineal cities and the areas of agricultural land they enclose. It is a theory that fits fairly neatly into an integrating Europe, and is one of many.

It could be said that no one has a safe cure for our expanding London but that it is a problem of a comprehensive nature resting upon a wide diversity of established fact. It cannot be solved, as we must be aware, by separately considered exercises related to housing, transport, industry, etc. It will not be solved by building only a New Town on the Isle of Sheppey. If it cannot be solved then our future is in jeopardy.

If we look further afield we will find everywhere the expanding problem reproduced. Paris, with its incisive form, its arterial articulation, its breadth and harmony, Paris, the loveliest city in the world, has at last succumbed to the pressure of numbers and faces death at the centre which was its life. The violent audacity of the solution known as Paris Parallèle showed how little the already

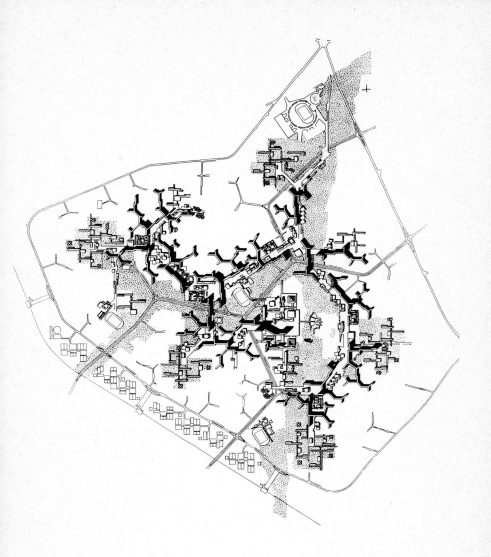

53 Le Mirail, town of 100,000,
five miles from Toulouse.
Competition site plan of 1961
by Candilis, Josic & Woods
shows apartment buildings
branching off continuous
pedestrian stem of communal
activity. The road systems are
separate.

54 A detail taken from the model of Kenzo Tange's Tokyo extension plan, showing the free relationship between road structure and building above the waters of Tokyo Bay.

55 The gathering of the road network of greater Tokyo into loopway system which is then projected into Tokyo Bay as a vast commercial and residential structure, relying heavily on the most advanced techniques but harking back to Japanese form. Kenzo Tange, architect.

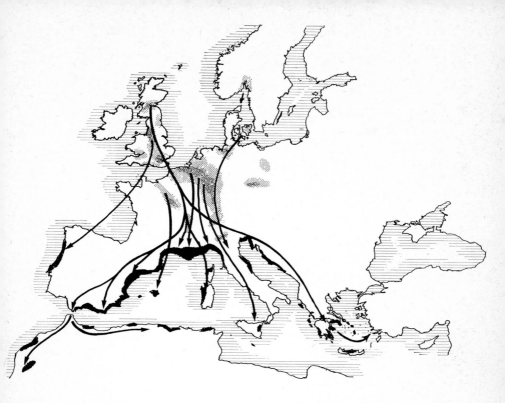

56 The flight of the workers to the sun. Diagram taken from the development plan of Gibraltar.

57 York Minster, from the walls of York. 'Looking inward to that cathedreal that remains substantially the largest single building in Yorkshire.'

58 Sheffield as it appeared 100 years ago before the increasing size of its factories and the number of its dwellings obliterated the form of the surrounding country.

59 Parkhill and Hyde Park housing developments, Sheffield, erected on the crests of hills from which the view of old Sheffield was taken, the slums having been cleared away from the slopes. The foreground is the subject of further civic development.

60 Woodside, one of several citadels of society, crowning the heights of Sheffield, from the slopes of which the last traces of an ignoble past are being expunged.

audacious autobahn system opening from the Porte d'Orleans was able to cope with the traffic alone, though the problem is not confined to traffic.

Elsewhere in France solutions take the form of new towns tacked on to old of which the extension of Toulouse, known as Toulouse le Mirail is much the most comprehensive and human. Its form, so interesting to the biologist, is in no way at variance with industry: it commands it, that is all.

But if we would experience the real shock of recognition we must study the various solutions to the problem of Tokyo's expansion put forward by Japanese architect-planners. There are no means of limiting the growth of Tokyo, says Kenzo Tange. The growth of cities is a phenomenon of technocracy coinciding with the decline of primary industries in England from 22 to 5 per cent, and the growth of tertiary industries, that is, of management, sales, finance, research from 30 to 62 per cent. The size of London has inevitably grown faster than the means of controlling it, and by these tokens Tokyo, which in 1960 had over thirteen million people in the metropolitan area, will number twenty million well before the turn of the century.

Tange makes the obvious point that the key to the working of such concentrations is communications, and the interesting rider to this is that personal communication 'between man and man, between man and function, and between function and function' are essential to success, the increase of *indirect* leading to a greater need of *direct* means of communication, without the intervention of any form of mechanical transmission. The London exchanges offer examples of the enduring forms of nevertheless very delicate organisations essentially based on the personal contact, the exchange of words, the steady glance in the eyes, of brokers dealing with 60 per cent of the world's cargoes, underwriting and arbitration. His radical scheme of renewal breaks the concentric and radial form that all great cities take if uncontrolled, and as Arthur Korn did in the Mars group plan of London in 1935, he creates a civic axis, a spine turning the city into an open system, based on a fascinating cyclical transport organisation which is too complicated to be explained in a few words.

What he has proposed is a structure, strange, complicated, of gargantuan scale, like no city we have ever before imagined (plates 54 and 55); yet I would say to you that it fits many of the facts of the Tokyo situation; it provides a definite and lasting base for the vital element of communication, and is structurally within our powers. Take it as a reflection of the gravity of the worlds urban problem, and its strangeness lessens.

The scheme of Noriaki Kuro Kaiva have a double interest for us. Like Tange's scheme it cuts a sort of axis through the concentric mass of Tokyo and makes for the shallow water of the bay, but its form, based upon I know not what system of construction, reverts to those of the vegetable kingdom. It appears in its fantastic and romantic way to express a longing for an entirely different way of life in which it is better to be a vegetable than a machine.

Look everywhere around at the cities of the world – Chicago, Baghdad, Mexico City, Buenos Aires, Lagos, Sydney, Calcutta, Cairo – wherever you look the phenomenon of uncontrolled growth repeats itself, rapid transit generating expansion that obliterates form, gradually overloads the radial arteries, and finally brings death to the centre.

Kenzo Tange's so-radical plan discloses the desperate nature of the Tokyo problem, but is at least a plan. For London there is as yet no more radical plan than there is for New York or Chicago or for most of the still expanding cities of the world, and I must ask you to think not only in terms of the dramatic central areas upon which we hope to practice a civil surgery of renewal, but of the areas, the limitless areas of urban penumbra that so recall White-head's description of the physical universe as being 'a dull affair, merely the hurrying of material, endlessly, meaninglessly' with the threat implicit in the connection of this 'spiritual nothingness' with that of atomic annihilation.

I speak of the plight of cities overcome by the sheer mass of their inhabitants, but we in Europe experience another blight that affects whole regions and is known as tourism. It is one form of the awakening of the masses to possess themselves of what formerly belonged to a minority. It is an expression of an abundance, the sign of rising standards of life, and the extension of possibilities of choice to lower levels of the population. It has risen in recent years to become a vast, seasonal migration following the sun, seeking health, entertainment and knowledge wherever they are to be had, but settling unfailingly upon what is old, beautiful, lichened, inconsequential, what is the reverse of the industrialised world from which it issues, but what, by being old and sensitive, unique and delicate, is unable to withstand the onslaught of mass appreciation and is destroyed by its very admirers (plate 56).

The extent of the damage done to the Mediterranean Riviera, the Costa Brava and the Island of Majorca is a foretaste of what will happen elsewhere as the immigration settles into a major industry dependent upon the exploitation of land for impermanent–permanent occupation. The Italian coastline has fallen, and now the hill sides, the very hill tops are invaded and the sense of contrast between the coast and the hills is becoming merged into the dull nothingness that our industrialised background has inured us to.

'You haven't been to Greece?' said my friend. 'Hurry my dear fellow, before it goes. Athens is already gone, and the Islands will follow soon.' The German girl in a bikini snapping the leaning tower of Pisa in technicolour has not a care in the world that has to do with this issue at least. She understands the matter as little as the clerk from Ealing jammed in his bright new Mini Minor in a Devon lane. But they *must* understand. They must co-operate in preservation or there will be nothing to preserve, for it is seldom imagined by anyone that we could create today what would be worth preserving in the future. If tourism is a stable feature of modern life then there is a potential that can be planned for, a movement that can be guided, and preservation may go hand in hand with creation.

Tourism is the sign of an awakening in the masses but it is not creative until it is confined and given a form as in some places it is. Brighton and Bath were alternative forms of pleasure town, and what could be nicer, there being no morality to be considered apart from the aesthetic of the necessary form of what is to be.

Tourism is industrialism at play, and once understood and catered for and its needs harmonised with those of agriculture, landscape and history it could take its place in the vital growth of Europe. It is as necessary in itself as the great industries that support it, and neither can continue to exist much longer in an unplanned state. Europe is now becoming a planning unit that overflows national boundaries. Our several countries have become too small for the potential that we feel within ourselves. So far from being decadent, so far from abdicating its authority as a power ruling from the centre of its inventive vitality, Europe moves towards the achievement of the form, both economic and political, that the release of new powers of production and communication open to it.

It is that form we are considering throughout this book and, in particular, that its evolution should be fashioned by a fuller use of the intuitive and comprehensive process, in place of the clumsy and restricted formuli mistakenly derived from the early discoveries of physical science.

Expo '67 in Montreal exposed the chronic nature of our impasse, for it was an exhibition without an objective, though it was supposed to concern people. Thus its national pavilions were on the whole mere technocratic show-offs, whatever went on inside, including the gargantuan golf-ball of the US pavilion and the drooping defeatist lines of the West German technocratic tent, both, like so much else, the manifestations of technique in search of substance. Only the brave and costly effort of Moshte Safte to square romance with technique in his cliff dwelling, Habitat, offered a possible solution to a pressing problem.

And so if there are to be more of these international exhibitions that are not mere commercial entertainments for the masses let them tell us something about our future. Or better still let us stage an exhibition here in England that does none other than that, that exposes the true nature of a future for environment, with every technocratic aid and apparatus in its subservient place.

The struggle to achieve form is waged between the conflicting outlooks of a technocracy that has become divorced from its roots in pure science, and one that is recalled through art to its ultimate purpose, which is to serve humanity. Thus the form we aim at is human, but the means of achieving it becomes increasingly mechanistic, and the question remains unsolved as to whether we can make a success of it, or whether, as many aver, the industrial system is based upon a false premise.

What increases our difficulties is sheer numbers. We are increasing population at a rate beyond our powers of nourishing it in body or in soul. We feel this pressure though we belong to a rich and stable country.

Yet despite the enormous damage of the last century and this, making it so much more difficult for us than for the Scandinavians or the Dutch to strike out a definite line for ourselves in the twentieth century, I can measure in my own working life a change in attitude that offers us a measure of hope.

Many years ago I went to Sheffield to lecture to the School of Architecture, and I remember stepping out from the railway station into a scene that prefigured hell. It was evening and the lights were coming on into a brown fog of rain and smoke, shot through by points of furnace glow. To the clatter of the streets was added the clanging of power hammers and the shrieks of bitten steel, and between sight and sound I was bewildered and overcome and remembered Sheffield thereafter with horror.

That was perhaps a quarter of a century ago, but in the last two years I have been several times to Sheffield, attracted by the first sight of the great Park Hill housing scheme looking down from its position on the hilltop over the scene I first encountered (plate 59), and then by the character of the then City Architect, Lewis Womersley, who had for the last ten years directed a reconstruction on a scale that opened the possibility of the national renewal that I had hoped for in the early days of modern architecture.

Sheffield is a city of about 600,000 inhabitants gathered into the folds of valleys running up on to the moors, and spreading out along the wider valleys of the Sheaf and Don and over land lying between them. It is a largish city but not too big to visualise and feel. You raise your eyes and there are hills above. Streams, in whatever sad state, flow somewhere near. It has configuration: you feel the moors. How power came to Sheffield I know not. Whether it was water power or iron ore that attracted men to it; but they settled in the valleys to make knives and scissors some time in the seventeenth or eighteenth century, and the opening markets of the world drove them on to add furnace to workshop, filling up the valleys in blind and inchoate urgency, houses and furnaces hugger-mugger, with no respect of nature or topography, roads finding their way where they could, up slopes or across them, the spaces crammed in with houses, the smallest possible, back-to-back, two up two down, with no sanitation, nor open space, no decency of anything, but shelters only. And the workshops were no better, places to get work done in, like the mills of Lancashire and Yorkshire, and the mines of Northumberland, like the great region of the Midlands, the Black Country under its permanent pall of smoke. Like the great material mind of England bent low under the hard yoke of material science, these workshops had to deny the spirit to fulfil the law of supply and demand.

Whatever form the city had was given it by the hills and valleys it blackened and befouled. The masters built in the valleys and as far up the slopes as economy allowed, and still the moors showed through; and the mass of it settled in and hardened, grew old, and saw bad times and good, and came at last to the unlovely present of ten years ago when Park Hill was first thought of.

Park Hill was thought of, you might say, by Gropius and le Corbusier, and the Mars Group, and by Ruskin and Morris, and by Blake, for there has hovered above all movements of reform in England the haunting possibility of 'a new Jerusalem in England. . . .' Thus, you may see the process of architectural creation exemplifying itself in a series of unified conceptions, each gathering a wide conspectus of contemporary events into a work of art with enduring elements, and not finite or closed, but rather offering itself to be fertilised further in works that gather new events in new circumstances.

Le Corbusier's dwelling unit at Marseilles, so rightly called l'Unité, made several practical proposals including the elaborate nursery school on the roof and the internal shopping street that were not of the greatest practical value. But the building, despite these defects, was in the spirit of its time, was at what y Gasset calls 'the height of its time'. It was moreover a work of religiously deep feeling and a work of lasting art deeply embedded in the contemporary spirit.

It must therefore have affected the works that equally affected the housing architects of Sheffield, and it is not the case only of formulas transmitted or skills acquired as it is the formation of an attitude, a taste or a culture, something that has no boundaries because it is, at base, a feeling.

The drama of the renewal of Sheffield centres about the confluence of the Sheaf and Don valleys where Sheffield began. But it extends everywhere, and notably in the valleys into which the black tide first moved.

One of the marvellous things about the Park Hill scheme is that not only the ridge tops on which it is built, but the steep slopes of the hillside itself were once covered with the most miserable dwellings man has ever conceived for himself, buildings born in sin and perpetuating sin. And these have gone. Park Hill looks over much inglorious city, but it looks down a new-born hillside upon which young trees are starting life.

And the same story is repeated in other valleys. The slopes leading up to the University were once encrusted with narrow streets of narrow houses with a sort of dour charm that is no more than the memory of the eighteenth century that was later to be expunged.

Some few remain to be replaced, and as they go a new life opens in the steps and courtyards of lovingly conceived new dwellings, and dramatically in great point blocks, each on its podium thrust forward into a rising band of parkway, marching upward towards the skyline of the moor.

At Woodside it is the hilltop that is crowned with a mixture of point blocks, blocks and lower buildings, the roads parting to leave the centre free for pedestrians to reach their houses up steps and ramps as in an Italian hill town, the lower edge ending abruptly in bastion-like blocks buttressed into the open space that everywhere sets a limit to building, defines it and gives it form, and charms the eye with variety and contrast, the very ingredients of art (plate 60).

So wherever one looks in this grim old city, the world's old workshop of knives and scissors, the hilltops are crowned with pleasure and delight, items in a rigorous housing policy, but something at last for William Blake to celebrate. And as each work is done the city gains in character, is individualised, separated out from the obfuscating mass of its former self, and achieves identity.

And this, my friends, is civilisation agitating the entropic mass to achieve identity. And the suburban apron of Detroit I described to you earlier is not civilisation, and no more are the formless seas of nameless occupation that wash up to the old hard core of eighteenth-century London.

But I have not done with Sheffield before I say something of the more rigorous problem at the centre where the two valleys meet. On one hillside there is Park Hill looking across the Sheaf valley to where the bulk of the administrative and commercial activities climb up the converse slope, soon to be embattled with a line of civic buildings, a continuous spine of law courts, library and art gallery, making a common face with the wall of the Technical College, overlooking the valley.

A third hill beyond the joining of the rivers rises in point blocks towards the emergent form of a new university.

Down in the valley bottoms still choked with nineteenth-century clutter run the railways and roads, and here in the new market centre, complicated in levels and merging new and old, taking in chain stores with rented stalls, and catering for all classes of citizens as a good market should, is the beginnings of a transformation that tests the weak nerves as it reaches for a statement of civic order engaging the full range of twentieth-century urban structure.

A main arterial motorway must sort itself out to near and far destinations; a railway, reduced soon to battle order, must discharge its function; cars and buses must be parked in great numbers; communal activities of sport and amusement must find a place, with housing to keep a life in all of it; and some spaces for the taking of breath and a change from activity. And so that each must act according to its virtue, which in road and railway alike is not to be mixed with, in car parks is to have accessible space, in housing is to be social, and in entertainment is to be gregarious; each function must be separated in plan or in level, or in both, the outcome of which is a sort of deck over the valley pierced at intervals for interchange of interlocking function, and above it all a high bridge connection between Park Hill and the city centre, bringing all the hill tops into the core of city life spread out below them.

All this, and more than I can describe in words that cover the full fling of it, is Sheffield's present state of renewal and it amounts to a new conception of life in the heart of industrial England, a life now measured in terms of human value, which is unmeasurable, but drawn out of the sinews of industry.

I say to the faint-hearted and those that despair of the state of art and culture, that here is a living art made up of an English town renewing itself, an art piled up of the very materials of living infused with the spirit of survival. So taken up is it with the spirit of living that it has no need to call itself art.

But if you would know how they feel about it listen to an Alderman coming into town with the City Architect: 'Spring'll be with us soon, Lewis. Look at the sun on the Woodside towers, lad. Does you good to see.'

I say once again that the aim of life is its continuation and that we continue where we find a form for life that allows it to exercise its functions harmoniously. That form is best expressed for us by the organisation of our life on the earth's face and for this we must adapt and modify the hard and resisting facts of nature to our ends and scrutinise her enigmatic face. This is the task of science.

But we must live ideally and religiously and for this we must lay ourselves open to revelation and await the intimations of immortality of which Wordsworth spoke. This is the way of art.

There was never a period of history when these two ends seemed further divorced, but late though the day is and great the damage done, the task that can harness these twin sides of our nature lies waiting in the reclamation of our country from the great error of its immediate past that has been making a desert of ignorant abstraction out of what was once realisable concrete form.

Do not imagine that these two sides of our nature are immediately capable of being merged into one indistinguishable attitude, but see them rather as fitted to different tasks, and find a discipline that will reconcile their difference in an over-all responsibility to society.

The day is late, not in Britain only, but everywhere over the world, where rising populations face the problem of successful survival, and our capacity to help these emergent nations rests now, I think, not so much on our accumulative skill as scientists and industrialists, not so much therefore on our past performance, as on the new combination of our contrasting faculties that we bring to the solution of this task of renewal. The way we do this task is what we have to teach, and this we have still to teach ourselves.

What Sheffield is doing for itself we must now set out to do for the whole of Britain, namely to harmonise the acts we perform in the image of an ideal form which is in fact the means whereby we continue. The dominant instrument in this task is an aspect of art but it is better to think of it as an attitude towards life.

We are, as I say, far from reaching this ideal, for even my own profession is too narrowly conceived to bear the weight of what it must carry out. If the recreation of our physical environment defines the chief end of architecture, then it must fail in performance unless it includes what also pertains to the building of towns, that is, civil and mechanical engineering, town planning, landscape architecture, sociology and so much else beside.

But what does this amount to, other than a complete reorientation of our attitude to education as the preparation for the task of social renewal in the light of a new appraisal of our responsibilities for what lies deeper than the economics or the materialist conception of any society, against which, as in Russia, its religious soul speaks through its young poets in chains?

If science would seek to prolong the domination it has so long exercised over the succeeding generations of our technocratic society; if economics could justify its importance in the affairs of life; if technocracy needs aims that will dignify its second-rate agitation, they must one and all abdicate their office, divest themselves of what glory still remains with them, and accept tasks subservient to comprehensive views of life heavy with the responsibilities of man for man.

There must then be banished for once and for all the misguided notion, which it is a temptation to fasten on to politicians because it is so obviously their political energiser, that numbers means progress, and that expansion is limitless. Whatever views are held about the universe they have no practical application for us here below, however difficult it is to combat this heady, but juvenile supposition.

So far from our universe expanding, it is of course contracting, as what was once unknown, speculative and limitless, is known, charted, partitioned and allotted, the ends of it no more than a day's travel away. That contraction is absolute.

When at the moment the word expanding is used, and nearly always attached to the universe, it is taken to mean that we too are expanding as though expansion was a form of progress, and creditable. And contracting is, contrariwise, deflating and discreditable. But with the contraction of the world, which we feel without as yet understanding it or having any reassuring emotions about it, appear ceilings of possibility concerned with population, food, use of land surface, communications of many kinds, water, rewards for effort, and so on, that appear ominous only if they are compared with the supposed other state.

Yet one of the difficulties in dealing with this so-called expanding universe is that its problems expand with us, and remain therefore unsolved. This is true of population, food and communications, and is not quite true of land, unless you are more than optimistic.

But if in place of the idea of chasing this endless expansion one takes note of its possible limitations, we replace the notion of progress as being an Olympic race with America and Russia in the lead, to one of filling out into the spaces of problems of limited extent, and the idea of progress is switched from being a linear thrust into the unknown, or an explosion into uncharted space, to being a fulfilment or an achievement the more possible to imagine as progress for having identifiable targets.

And almost at once value judgements are in question; and these are our concern. It is as though we switched from basing our life on a sales campaign backed by a productivity drive, to the fulfilment, however difficult of achievement or idealistic in essence, of a mission.

Many years ago Sir Frank Pick, the general manager of London's buses and underground system, who was a man of as moral and idealistic a nature as Lord Reith, told me how confined he was by the commercial expansionist nature of the undertaking he served:

> I am not allowed to be responsible for my acts. If I drive a new tube extension into the open land, as it was, to Cockfosters, I generate an explosion of development that contained by town planning becomes a community of value; or left to care for itself, is a matter of numbers only, a proliferation without identity.

And this is the problem that Henry Adams weighed in trying to assess what he first took proudly to be the really explosive nature of American expansion, and had eventually to set beside the infinitely more productive output of the twelfth and thirteenth century of the Île de France, registered in the cathedrals of that area.

And so I felt when I walked along the walls of York looking inward to that cathedral that remains substantially the largest single building in Yorkshire. 'This building,' I said to myself, my eyes wandering lovingly about the delicate and meaningful articulations of its great mass, 'is of the utmost quality; first-class in whatever it set out to do. It is not only the audacious engineering of it, the pure thought taken for the thrusts of its downward pressures, but the containment of them in stone form the celebration of the act, the architecture. And of what supports this architecture; the glory of the glass telling the same story of suffering and hope that we must come again to know; the carving; the iron work; the books of hours; the treasured missals.'

This, I mused, was no work of anonymity, however submerged into the one transcendental idea appear now to be the contributions of its authors. Men such as Henry Yvele were brought in, men of substance and consequence. And at that time how many other cathedrals, what abbeys and monasteries beside competed for the services of the architects, artists and craftsmen of this quality that at any period of history, encouraged by whatsoever rewards, temporal or spiritual, must always be in short supply?

Then I stepped down into the city and opened the doors on a dozen parish churches, on guild halls and almshouses, the remains of chantries; and in the perceptible graduation of quality from the Minster downward I got some sense of measurement of effort, of some direction or polarisation of it towards a sustaining ideal, the filling out from market-day parish-mindedness to the City of God.

Then I thought of what was contained within the city walls, of the dangerous waste land of warring England beyond, against which these walls sheltered a population so small* by our measurement that even granted the gentler pace of events over the centuries of

* The population of York in the year 1200 is estimated to have been little more than 10,000.

mediaeval building, the sheer weight and mass of it must be accounted for, and its spiritual significance marvelled at and laid at the door of this community.

And if life was as short and brutish as we in our complacency suppose, why then did they everywhere celebrate it as they did; and not only the life to come, but the life that was lived to aspire to it?

And if life was short and brutish how long, how peaceful and unbrutish is life for so many in this violent present? moving towards what further violence? what unidealistic future?

As we contemplate this mystery of mediaeval York we move into what opens for us as a choice of ways, for I believe with Geoffrey Vickers that our major problems can no longer invite technocratic solutions because those we seek are in essence cultural and political. Even more rigorously, that we must make a choice, final and irrevocable, between a future, technocratic and explosive in nature, or one that is contained by what concerns us as societies of human beings aspiring towards possibilities of fulfilment.

What could defeat us then would be neither technocracy nor materialism, but the eternal conflict that takes place between the two sides of our nature, a conflict submerged by three hundred years of false promise, we now envisage – face to face as is the true meaning of that word – as being both the misery and the hope for a distracted world.

Index